Praise for *Life In Community*

A practical, engaging book on the indispensable role a healthy local church plays in reaching its community. Willis shows us why the local church is God's "plan A," the table, Willis says, He sets with grace for all who are hungry. Willis's style makes for easy reading, all the while hammering you with great gospel insights. You'll be entertained and motivated through this short, compelling book!

J. D. GREEAR, pastor of The Summit Church, Raleigh-Durham, North Carolina, author, *Gaining by Losing: Why the Future Belongs to Churches That Send*

I am grateful for this book, for it provides us this picture of the church that we desperately need to see in our day. Taken straight from Scripture, then buttressed with poignant illustrations and practical application, these pages drip with the depth of community that Christ has designed for His church.

DAVID PLATT, president of the International Mission Board, author of *Radical, Follow Me*, and *Counter Culture*

Life in Community is just the sort of call every Western Christian needs in this age of individualism, consumerism, and compartmentalization. Dustin Willis's treatment of community's role in the Christian life is balanced, biblical, and well-timed.

MATT CARTER, pastor of preaching, Austin Stone Community Church, coauthor, *The Real Win*

The church of the Lord Jesus Christ is a community of repenting sinners bonded together in a blood covenant in Jesus Christ. We are called to live, not in isolation but with one another. As a family community, we share certain values and commitments under the lordship of Jesus Christ. *Life In Community* fleshes this out in a manner that is biblically faithful, theologically rich, and practically helpful. This is a book that will serve well any church that wants to be an authentic biblical community.

DANIEL L. AKIN, president of Southeastern Baptist Theological Seminary, author of *A Theology for the Church*

Dustin's conviction to see local churches reach their full potential pours off the pages. He lives what he sees Scripture prescribe. *Life in Community* will calibrate the hearts of God's people to His mission for our daily lives.

D. A. HORTON; author of *G.O.S.P.E.L.* and national coordinator of Urban Student Missions at the North American Mission Board

God created us to be in community. He also created the church—the community we desire. Through Jesus, he made us part of that community. The community is strong, our membership secure. Even so, we struggle to actively participate in that community. With the heart of a pastor, Dustin encourages us and shows us how to engage in Jesus' community—the community we need and desire—for our good and God's glory.

ELLIOT GRUDEM, lead pastor for church planting and leadership development, Vintage Church

We live in an increasingly isolated world. In *Life in Community* Dustin Willis gets to the core of what it takes to build a community that brings the power of the gospel to the heart of that isolation. If applied, Dustin's message won't just lead to deeper, more meaningful relationships within the church but to a thoroughly biblical manner of pursuing God's mission in North America and beyond.

KEVIN EZELL, president of the North American Mission Board, SBC

Dustin has captured the heartbeat of what people look for in the local church: a safe place to walk with God in the context of biblical family. *Life in Community* gives us a picture of what the local church should look like when it's known by its love.

DHATI LEWIS, lead pastor of Blueprint Church, Atlanta, Georgia

In *Life in Community* Dustin challenges us to see that biblical community and missional effectiveness cannot be separated. He provides a helpful and much-needed reminder that engaging in God's mission of redemption is in a fact a communal activity.

BRAD BRISCO, author of *Missional Essentials* and *The Missional Quest*

Only the gospel forms Christian community, people formed together because Christ has rescued them. And community that is really Christian always results in mission—in people advancing the gospel together. I am grateful for Dustin's work and helpful challenge.

ERIC GEIGER, vice president, LifeWay Christian Resources, coauthor of *Simple Church*

Life in Community encourages us to realize our basic need and the incredible blessings that occur when we live in community. Dustin clearly motivates us to pursue authentic community with the understanding that is terribly messy and wonderfully beautiful at the same time. More importantly, *Life in Community* helps us realize that the quest for community will often magnetically draw others toward God.

MARY FRANCES BOWLEY, founder, chief strategic officer of WellSpring Living, author of *The White Umbrella*

So many in the church, even in church leadership, draw a tacit distinction between community and evangelism—one is inside the church and the other is outside. But what if that's a false distinction and actually undermines the mission of the church? Dustin Willis does a wonderful job of helping believers see how to do the mission of church in community, in homes, in friendship, in relationship. *Life in Community* is a resource that can help any church.

BARNABAS PIPER, blogger, podcaster, and author of *The Pastor's Kid* and *Help My Unbelief*

Our culture is more connected but more lonely than ever before. Wow!!! If Dustin's insights could ripple through the church, our lives and future generations would be better for it!

CLAY SCROGGINS, lead pastor of North Point Community Church

Genuine gospel community is sadly missing in the church today. This is why Dustin Willis calls us to return to the biblical model of experiencing relationships that are truly engaging and openly authentic. *Life in Community* will help you leave the dangerous waters of personal isolationism and transition into the tranquil waters of gospel community that results in life change and overflowing hope.

RONNIE FLOYD, president, Southern Baptist Convention and senior pastor, Cross Church

Community for many people—both inside and outside the church—is a dream that often goes unrealized. We strive to be known, and long for authentic relationships, but often it feels like life in community is nearly impossible. In *Life in Community*, Dustin Willis paints a practical picture of community with excellence, while marrying a biblical and gospel-centered foundation for life together as Christians. I'm particularly grateful for his attention to the inseparability of community and mission. This is an excellent book!

TODD ENGSTROM, executive pastor of Ministries, Austin Stone Community Church

I am struck often by Jesus' prayer for us to be unified together as believers. His intention is for our community to both nourish us and to invite outsiders to know His nourishing love for them. Heart-level community is a foundational ingredient in the gospel transforming insiders and outsiders, which is why I'm thrilled Dustin Willis has written this book. He gives us key ingredients for building lasting and impactful community.

CHRISTINE HOOVER, author of *The Church Planting Wife* and *From Good to Grace*

I absolutely loved *Life in Community*. I highly recommend this for every small group if they want to grow in how they relate to one another. It's clear, simple, and extremely practical.

BOB ROBERTS JR., senior pastor of NorthWood Church, author of *Bold as Love*

Today's individualistic culture needs community. A true community that resembles the love of Jesus to the world. Dustin challenges readers to view the church as a table, embracing each other, loving one another, and simply living together in order to do the mission of Jesus in this world. Readers will be challenged to no longer view the world as a lonely place, but rather a true church living out Acts 2 as one missional family.

KEVIN NGUYEN, pastor of Saddleback Church, Irvine, CA

Life in Community

Joining Together to Display the Gospel

DUSTIN WILLIS

MOODY PUBLISHERS
CHICAGO

Edited by Ginger Kolbaba
Interior design: Erik M. Peterson
Cover design: Marcus Williamson and Erik M. Peterson
Cover photo: Landon Jacob Productions

All websites and phone numbers listed herein are accurate at the time of publication but may change in the future or cease to exist. The listing of website references and resources does not imply publisher endorsement of the site's entire contents. Groups and organizations are listed for informational purposes, and listing does not imply publisher endorsement of their activities.

Some names within the text have been changed to protect the individuals' privacy.

Library of Congress Cataloging-in-Publication Data

Willis, Dustin.
   Life in community : joining together to display the gospel / Dustin Willis.
      pages cm
   ISBN 978-0-8024-1332-1 (paperback)
   1. Communities--Religious aspects--Christianity. 2. Church. 3. Christian communities.
   4. Evangelistic work. I. Title.
   BV625.W55 2015
   253--dc23
                        2015008408

We hope you enjoy this book from Moody Publishers. Our goal is to provide high-quality, thought-provoking books and products that connect truth to your real needs and challenges. For more information on other books and products written and produced from a biblical perspective, go to www.moodypublishers.com or write to:

Moody Publishers
820 N. LaSalle Boulevard
Chicago, IL 60610

1 3 5 7 9 10 8 6 4 2

Printed in the United States of America

DEDICATION

To my family: Renie, Jack, and Piper. You have sacrificed so much for this work. I am blessed to build community with the greatest missions team I will ever lead. I love you guys. May we continue to invite others to the table.

CONTENTS

FOREWORD

Christ and His church are the only cure for the crisis of loneliness that characterizes our culture.

To some, that may sound like an overstatement, but I make it without qualification. In fact, I would go a step further to say that Christ and His church are the only cure for crisis rampant loneliness that characterizes *every* culture. And there is a crisis. In a world where we are more connected technologically than we have ever been, at the same time we are more isolated personally than we have ever been. As a result, we desperately need to rediscover the depth of community God has designed for each of us in Christ as members of His church.

The problem, however, is that we're confused about community when it comes to the church. The majority of people in America associate a church with a physical building. "Where is your church?" people may ask, or "Where do you go to church?" And we don't just identify buildings as churches; we also classify churches according to the programs they offer. This church has a creative children's program, that church has a cool student ministry, these churches have great resources for married couples, and those churches have helpful group meetings for people who are divorced. Churches often revolve around programs for every age and stage of life.

Association and identification of the church with buildings and programs reflects an overtly consumer-driven, customer-designed approach that we have devised for attracting people to the "church." In order to have an effective, successful "church," we need an accessible building with nice grounds and convenient parking. Once people get to the building, we need programs that are customized for people's children, music that is attractive to people's tastes, and sermons that are aimed at people's needs. When taken to the extreme, this means that when people come to "church," they need a nice parking space, a latte waiting for them when they walk through the door, a themed preschool ministry with a custom-built slide, a state-of-the-art program that provides entertainment for teenagers, a topnotch band that plays great music, and a feel-good presentation by an excellent preacher who wraps things up in a timely fashion at the end of the morning.

But is all of this what God had in mind when He set up His church? Better put, is any of this what God had in mind when He set up His church? Identification of churches with buildings may seem common to us, but it's foreign to the New Testament, where we never once see the church described as a physical building. Similarly, the New Testament never once portrays the church as a conglomeration of customized programs. So much of what we associate with the church today is extrabiblical at best (it *adds* to what God's Word says) and unbiblical at worst (it *undercuts* what God's Word says).

When you turn through the pages of the New Testament, you see a very different picture of the church. Instead of a building, you see a body made up of members and a family made up of brothers and sisters. Biblically, a church doesn't consist of people who simply park and participate in programs alongside one another. Instead, the church comprises people who share the life of Christ with each other on a day-by-day, week-by-week basis.

After all, this is the pattern that was set between Jesus and His disciples from the beginning. Jesus loved these twelve men, served them, taught them, encouraged them, corrected them, and journeyed through life with them. He spent more time with these twelve disciples than He did with everyone else in his ministry put together. They walked together along lonely roads; they visited together in crowded cities; they sailed and fished together on the Sea of Galilee; they prayed together in the desert and on the mountains; and they worshiped together in the synagogues and at the temple. During all of this time together, Jesus taught them how to live and showed them how to love as He shared His life with them.

It makes sense, then, to see the rest of the New Testament envision a church as a group of Christ followers living alongside one another for the sake of one another. According to Scripture, the church is a community of Christians who care for one another, love one another, host one another, receive one another, honor one another, serve one another, instruct one another, forgive one another, motivate one another, build peace with one another, encourage one another, comfort one another, pray for one another, confess sin to one another, esteem one another, edify one another, teach one another, show kindness to one another, give to one another, rejoice with one another, weep with one another, hurt with one another, and restore one another. All of these "one anothers" combined together paint a picture not of people who come to a building filled with customized programs but of people who have decided to lay down their lives to love one another.

This is the kind of love we all need, and this is the kind of life for which we were all designed. Life in community. The kind of community where we can share and listen, teach and learn, laugh and cry. The kind of community where we're able to sincerely hurt and genuinely help. The kind of community where any one of us can belong and all of us will be loved. The kind of community where every single one of us can experience the joy of knowing our Creator while thriving in the purpose for which He created us. In other words, the kind of community God has created us to find in Christ and His church alone.

I am grateful for this book, for it provides us this picture of the church that we desperately need to see in our day. Taken straight from Scripture, then buttressed with poignant illustrations and practical application, these pages drip with the depth of community that Christ has designed for His church. Moreover, every chapter intentionally connects the beauty of community with the urgency of mission, calling us to pursue community not simply for our own good, but for the good of others. This book rightly shows the relationship between the local body of Christ and the global mission of God.

In addition, I am grateful for this author. Dustin Willis has not just written these words; he lives these words. I praise God for the humility with which he writes as a follower of Christ, and the authenticity with which he lives in community with others.

—DAVID PLATT

INTRODUCTION

For as long as I can remember, the wooden table was a part of our home. There was nothing special about it—it was old, cracked, and broken—but around that table my family laughed and cried, fought and forgave. On it we shared meal after meal.

Honestly though, I really didn't think much about the table until the day I brought my girlfriend, Renie, home for the first time. She was there to meet my family and I found myself filled with a strange emotional concoction of fear and terror.

The food was all there: fried catfish, mashed potatoes with gravy (of course), green beans, macaroni and cheese (not the creepy kind in the box), biscuits, and sweet tea.

The family was all there too: the almost funny jokes, the unbelievable stories that you really had to be there for, the sports commentary on our favorite ball team, and details about the latest medical test that you really wish you could "un-hear."

At some point during dinner I realized the table wasn't just a table. It was a point of meeting—a beautiful site where the people I call "family" shared our lives. There our scattered and hectic worlds were forged in oneness. At that table we experienced life in community.

The beauty of the table caused my fear to turn to joy. I wanted my future wife to experience this table. I wanted "my" table to become "our" table.

The church is meant to be a table. The good news of Jesus declares that not only has the sin that separated us from God been removed but also the barriers that divided us from one another (Eph. 2:11–22). All those who are in Christ are united into one really big family with God Himself as our Father. The church, then, gathers as a family around God's table.

- There we celebrate together through the joys of life;
- There we weep together through the pain that life brings;
- There we confess sin and fight for holiness;
- There we serve one another as we meet needs and bear burdens;
- There we encourage one another to follow Christ no matter the cost.

This table is a compelling missionary power in the life of the church. When we are living life in community we long for others to share in this experience. "Come, meet my big, crazy, messed up, beautiful extended family," we say. "There you will find the love, care, and burden-bearing relationships for which you crave."

Perhaps at some time in your life you've found yourself in a new location. You were alone—or at least that's how you felt. You longed for someone to notice you and invite you into their lives. You wanted a table. You needed the church.

Thankfully there is no need to separate community and mission. In the brilliance of God's design, these two function in tandem. Jesus, in fact, prayed for this in John 17. He begs the Father "that they may become perfectly one, so that the world may know that you sent me and loved them even as you loved me" (John 17:23). Jesus links the love that we have with one another with His mission to the world. As we grow in love for one another, the world will be drawn to saving faith.

That's what life in community is all about—the power of gospel-centered communities in a lonely world. With a table marked by love our cities can be transformed.

My family recently moved into a neighborhood in suburban Atlanta. Vince and Darlene live just a couple streets over from our house. They have three sons and little to no background in the church. Vince said he used to go to church as a kid but the service was in Spanish and of course, he knows zero Spanish. This couple has become our best friends. We eat together, laugh together, vacation together, serve our city together, and discuss the gospel together in a small group that meets weekly. This past Christmas, Vince and Darlene had all of our small group families over to their home where they cooked an elaborate meal and then sat us all down by the Christmas tree and gave everyone, including our kids, a very personal and thoughtful gift. Afterwards Vince paused and said to us, "We wanted to do this for you because in some way, we just needed to show you our appreciation. We have never had anything like this before. This is more than just friendship. I don't know what all of this means but I know that you guys are our family and there is something different here that I have not really had before. I don't know if I believe what you believe yet, but the way you guys treat and love one another is just different. We love you guys! Merry Christmas."

What a gift, right? The crazy thing is these words didn't come from the mouth of a mature Christian. Vince and Darlene are still seeking. They have, however, observed firsthand the beauty of the table and they find it compelling.

God's design is for His table to be found everywhere: on college campuses, in middle-class living rooms and urban apartment complexes, and across developing countries. Imagine the possibilities of what could be and should be: countless gospel communities scattered around the world—New York, Vancouver, London, Small Town U.S.A., Tokyo, San Francisco, Atlanta's suburbs, the mountains of Nepal, Tehran, and Siem Reap, Cambodia—all caring for one another and serving the city where God has placed them. This is the table God has called us to!

Recapture the wonder of community marked by the gospel and moved by the Spirit; pull up a seat to the table and experience life in community.

FORMING COMMUNITY

"By this all people will know that you are my disciples, if you have love for one another."

—JESUS (JOHN 13:35)

CHAPTER 1

THE NEED
FOR COMMUNITY

Loneliness.

I t's a heavy word. One that everyone feels but no one wants to admit. Something in us longs for the connection we have when we sit at a meal with those we love. There we experience abundant food, authentic relationships, laughter, and tears. We are fully known and fully loved. We wish that we could spend all of life around that table, but often we feel that we just can't get there. We want community, yet we struggle with loneliness.

As a pastor, I've heard countless heartbreaking stories of people wallowing in loneliness. My friend Jay, for instance, spent ten years living in New York City. He was surrounded by people yet, by his own admission, he was the loneliest he'd ever been. He told me, "Proximity with twenty-five million people does not equal community."

Or take Nicki who grew up in a big family. Each Sunday they plastered on smiles as they entered the church building, but Monday through Saturday, Nicki lived in a horrific prison that her parents called a home. One of the first things Nicky shared with me was that she had been lonely as long as she could remember.

Or there's the married couple who attended a church I pastored. One evening I listened as they poured out their struggles, seemingly unable to zero in on the cause of their frustrations. These two people, whom most would refer to as the life of the party, confessed that they

We live in the most connected time in world history, yet as a society we are as isolated as we have ever been.

each struggled with intense isolation. Loneliness can challenge church leaders as well. On countless nights during a season of incredible church growth, I felt as though no one really knew or even cared about me. Each week I'd preach three services in a row to capacity crowds, and then get in my car and aimlessly drive around, wondering why I felt so alone. I was connected to thousands of people, yet I struggled with an overwhelming sense of separation.

Isolation has no prejudice. It will seek you out regardless of whether you live in a small town or the big city, earn millions or barely make minimum wage, rarely attend church or are a pastor. It attacks all people at all times.

MORE SOCIAL THAN SOCIAL MEDIA

We live in the most connected time in world history, yet as a society we are as isolated as we have ever been. Two hundred and twenty-two million US adults can connect with the world from any location with the touch of a button. Cellphones make it possible to talk to someone without being present, and we can text without ever hearing a person's voice. We are constantly linked through Facebook, Twitter, Snapchat, Pinterest, Instagram (and whatever else some Ivy League student creates next week).

Technology has made communication so easy that we are addicted to convenience. Sadly even with all this amazing technology, it is more difficult than ever for us to build genuine relationships. In a *Newsweek* interview, John T. Cacioppo, a neuroscientist at the University of Chicago, stated: "Social-networking sites like Facebook may provide people with a false sense of connection that ultimately increases loneliness in people who feel alone. These sites should serve as a supplement, but not replacement for, face-to-face interaction."[1]

These advances—while not bad in and of themselves—have the

potential to lead us into more isolated lonesomeness, especially when we replace authentic, vulnerable, face-to-face relationships with more-controlled, less-genuine social media ones.

Recently I overheard someone in a coffee shop sharing weight loss ideas. "Every time you feel the urge to eat, crunch ice instead," the man told his companion. He explained that the sensation of chewing and consuming the ice would help soothe the urge to want to eat. "It's a way to trick your body."

That is the dumbest thing I've ever heard, I thought. Dumb or not, sure enough, a couple days later I found myself trying it. (Just getting back to my fighting weight, you know.) I discovered that while ice is good for cooling a drink, in the end it doesn't supply the sustainable nourishment that my body needs. And chewing ice certainly doesn't fulfill noshing on something more satisfying and lasting. It works only for a brief moment.

Likewise, social media tricks our society into believing that it can give us what we need. But really it fails to be a sustainable means of community. We think we are growing strong bonds of friendship, while we spend inordinate amounts of time reading posts and updates from others who make us aware that everybody else has a cooler life than we do. We may think it will satisfy our loneliness, but the reality is that it only manages to deepen it.

HOW LONELY ARE WE, REALLY?

Any person can make "friends" through social media, but when was the last time you had a conversation with someone who genuinely cared for you and meaningfully spoke into your life? Far too many Americans offer an alarming answer to that question. Recent studies from Duke University and the US Census suggest that our society is in the midst of the most dramatic and progressive slide toward disconnection in history. Consider these disturbing statistics:

- 27.2 million people live alone.
- More people say they *feel alone* than at any other time.

- 25 percent say they have no one they can turn to as a confidant.
- More people link their depression to loneliness.
- The number of "socially isolated" Americans has doubled since 1985.[2]

Not only are more people physically living alone, they are becoming emotional lone rangers. Since they have no one to turn to, they seek the individualistic dreams that ultimately cripple human flourishing and societal progress. Rick Warren summed it up well: "Isolation exists because we have a culture that feeds individualism. The fruit of rampant individualism in our culture is massive loneliness."[3]

> God Himself placed within us this yearning for community—a God-given appetite for honest connection with others.

Instead of sitting on the porch and talking with neighbors and friends as it was in the "good ole days," often we now enter our homes as the garage door closes behind us, and surrounded by our privacy fence, we eat dinner alone and then vicariously live out community by watching television "reality" shows (as our neighbors do the same).

Yet even in our chosen solitude, we have insatiable need for connection. Give us two seconds of down time and we reach for our phone to scan Twitter, Facebook, and Instagram feeds.

You can even see our desire for community through our television viewing choices. Some of the highest-rated shows over the past thirty years include *Cheers*, *Seinfeld*, *Friends*, and *Parks & Rec*. Each show represents what the 1980s' classic *Cheers* communicates in its theme song: "Sometimes you want to go where everybody knows your name" or as *Friends* references, "I'll be there for you."

Those are not empty lyrics but rather an outcry from culture. We are part of a civilization that starves for unpretentious relationships with others who genuinely care and can share in life's common struggles. These shows are not reality. Life is not one continuous dance in a fountain with our closest friends. Nonetheless these shows strike a felt need.

People want real community. We yearn to be part of a community that discovers and clings to identity, worth, and value.

It's as if watching these sitcoms gives us a taste of what it would be like to have genuine relationships with people who not only know our name but who know us and are willing to struggle with us.

A BETTER ANSWER

Despite our inherent longing, many of us feel that sense of belonging is somehow unattainable. We desire it, but we resist it at the same time. We fear being transparent with others. What if we get hurt? Rejected? Betrayed? Ignored? Neglected?

The answer the world might give to this conundrum is simply for us to find people we like and trust, then try to work on our issues (whatever that means). It's a self-improvement, *pull yourself up from your bootstraps* mentality.

Christians have a profoundly different answer to this longing, which we find in the good news of Jesus Christ. We know that God Himself placed within us this yearning for community—a God-given appetite for honest connection with others. The idyllic garden of Eden with its unbroken relationships haunts us because that's what we were designed for (see Gen. 2:18; Rom. 5:10). But as our self-centered sin entered the picture, that perfection was lost—traded for the brokenness and despair we feel from being disconnected from God and one another (see Gen. 3).

Yet God did not leave us there. He created a history-sweeping work to redeem us, to restore the wholeness of Eden. That redeeming work happens through the church—the people whom, through Christ's death and resurrection, God has rescued from their own folly (see Eph. 2:1–10). He has taken a bunch of traitors and adopted us into His family, welcoming us to His table (see Gal. 4:4–7; Rev. 19:6–9). God has made us a community with a deeper foundation and a brighter future than anything the world has to offer.

During the time I struggled with loneliness, it was through community that the pockets of emptiness began to fill. Many argue that Jesus is all we need. While I agree that Jesus alone is all we need for salvation, I find throughout the Bible that the Christian life is designed to be lived with other believers. From the outset God told us, "It is not good that the man should be alone" (Gen. 2:18). Moreover, in all the letters the apostle Paul wrote, he specifically gave communal instruction for how to live the Christian life: love one another, serve one another, confess your sins to one another, etc.

When I battled loneliness, restoration didn't magically and immediately occur, and it didn't happen on its own. I had to be honest with others and then be willing to listen and soak in their words of blunt truth and timely encouragement.

God's Word speaks in a direct, relevant, and timely way to the tension that resides between people's desire for relationships and their inability to sustain those relationships. As the church we are called not only to seek the lost, we are called to bring hope and help to relationships, to minister to people's loneliness. To do that, we must contend for a community defined by the Scriptures, rather than fall into the counterfeit pattern of individualism that is so prevalent in the world (and that too often sneaks into our churches).

Throughout Scripture we see the power and importance of community. In John 17:20–23, for instance, Jesus prayed for the unity of the believers, while in John 13:35, He said the world would know that the disciples were His by how they loved one another.

Even Jesus' instruction for evangelism and mission were all given to a community of tight-knit believers—not simply to individuals (see Matt. 28:19; John 20:21; Acts 1:8). These types of communities bring hope to a lonely and isolated society. In fact, our entire lives are meant to be lived in community on mission (see Eph. 2:1–22).

Often when I speak of community, I find that people believe they are already walking in healthy community. But as I ask them to dig deeper, I find that they have a set time and place (often on Sunday) when they meet together, but they are not by any means digging beyond the surface into the matters of the heart.

Community is an incredible gift God has given us to experience, but because of our tendency toward individualism, the real thing is often far from our reach. With God's gracious pursuit and some intentionality, however, we can recover it in all its fullness.

AN UNNECESSARY DIVIDE

For many churches, the idea of community usually takes the form of a small group. Many of these small groups follow a specific type of structure, whether cell groups, Sunday school classes, life groups, or some other clever name they've brainstormed to emphasize Christian community. Alongside these community-focused groups, churches have also concluded that they are designed to engage in missions (at least I hope they have).

Though missions and groups are assumed staples within the church, the depth of community often varies. These strategies have often, inadvertently, created a divide between the mission to reach those outside the church and the mission to connect individuals in the church to one another. Most churches are good at one or the other.

Some churches pride themselves in being a loving church, meaning that they care well for one another. Often these churches struggle to reach out to new people because they might mess up the fellowship that the body cherishes. Other churches pride themselves in reaching out to those who are far from God. Often these churches struggle to connect new Christians to genuine relationships where they can grow in Christlikeness.

Church researchers Tim Chester and Steve Timmis have discovered that

> As people live on mission with others, they discover community. And as people live in true community, they will seek mission.

Western culture has become very compartmentalized. We want to spend more time in evangelism, but because this can happen only at the expense of something else, it never happens.

Rethinking evangelism as relationship rather than event radically changes this. . . . Our identity as human beings is found in community. Our identity as Christians is found in Christ's new community. And mission takes place through communities of light. . . . Christian community is a vital part of a Christian's mission. Mission takes place as people see our love for one another.[4]

Do mission and community have to be separated? No. We must aggressively fight against the false idea that community happens over in one area while mission and evangelism take place separately within their own space or program. When this duality exists, the church's effectiveness is diminished severely because it compartmentalizes our lives as believers.

How do we pursue community and mission? It's more closely connected than you may realize. As people live on mission with others, they discover community. And as people live in true community, they will seek mission. Community and mission are not in competition with each other—they are inseparable. You don't have to choose one or the other.

If you have ever been on a mission trip then you know what I'm talking about. You return from the trip having never felt closer to a group of people or more inspired to be involved in God's work. For many churches, mission trips are the only place that Christian community and intentional mission intersect. Why is the environment created through mission trips not the culture that daily permeates our churches?

Eliminating the duality that exists in missions and community and melding these ideas together will help spread the gospel to a lonely world. Not only do gospel communities act as a beacon of light but they also become a place of healing for the soul.

MISSION THROUGH COMMUNITY

Gospel communities alone do not bring about identity and worth, but they display the One who does. God has reconciled believers to

Himself. Gospel community is a means to exhibit the gospel's light to a dark and hurting society (see Matt. 5:14–16).

"The most persuasive argument for the Christian faith is the Christian community," notes Todd Engstrom, executive pastor at Austin Stone Community Church. "The majority of conversions throughout church history have come not through argumentation, but through belonging to a meaningful community before belief is ever required."[5]

What would it look like if our communities were united by this hope-filled gospel, actively loving and caring for one another as they live out mission together? Acts 2:46–47 gives us an indication: "Day by day, attending the temple together and breaking bread in their homes, they received their food with glad and generous hearts, praising God and having favor with all the people. And the Lord added to their number day by day those who were being saved."

Communities centered on the gospel fly in the face of isolation and yet convey the grace-filled inclusion that we so desperately desire. These communities bring with them the answer the world is hungry for. It is a community that invites others to feast at the Lord's table.

Picture it: a community for the hurting, the lonely, the has-beens, the have-nots, the accomplished, the rebellious, the self-righteous. Picture God taking this ragtag group and forming them together for the greatest mission we could ever join. This is His track record from Genesis to now.

Community is more than a Sunday and mission is more than a trip. Discovering and building this idea may seem overwhelming, but through the Holy Spirit's work, it is possible. Through gospel community, we can eradicate the epidemic of individualism and loneliness. I have experienced it and have watched as God has done this in thousands of others' lives.

Why does life in community matter? That's what we're about to discover. Through the pages of this book we'll explore the power and importance of doing life together, we'll dig into what that should look like, and we'll make a proactive plan for how we will pursue intentionally living that way. Are you ready to be part of the exciting adventure of life in community? Let's go!

GETTING PRACTICAL

- **WHEN** was the last time you had a deep, heart-level conversation with another believer? What has been the challenge in pursuing that? Would you commit to scheduling a time to talk with a fellow believer and go deeper?
- **DOES** heart-level conversation happen regularly with a consistent group of people (ideally from your local church)?
- **WHEN** was the last time you had meaningful conversation over a meal at your house? At someone else's?
- **HOW** many of your neighbors do you know more intimately than by merely saying, "Hey, how's it going?"
- **HOW** many people know the real struggles you face? To what degree?

Life in Community

"I appeal to you therefore, brothers, by the mercies of God, to present your bodies as a living sacrifice, holy and acceptable to God, which is your spiritual worship."

—ROMANS 12:1

CHAPTER 2

COMMON GROUND

Damon was short, exceedingly nonathletic, and a genius. Gene was tall, tremendously athletic, and couldn't care less about academics. Damon liked everyone, had no enemies, and loved to be with people. Gene didn't care for anyone, had a lot of enemies, and never worried about what anyone thought of him. Damon was an electrical engineer who loved to cook—to the point that, in his spare time, he earned a degree in culinary arts. Gene was a bouncer in the local clubs and loved to hit people in the face (thirteen counts of aggravated assault), and eventually, in his spare time, learned mixed martial arts. Damon sought career-based success because he wanted to fulfill a desire for acceptance and approval. Gene rebelled against the societal norms in hopes of finding some type of power and control that always seemed to escape him.

Though Damon and Gene were different in every way, they shared two things in common: their search for worth and their need of a Savior.

When these two men became Christians, they also became part of the same community, for now these two polar-opposite men had common ground: growing in their faith and walking the path of Jesus' mission for the church.

Damon and Gene are not all that unusual in the body of Christ. After all, more things seem to separate us than bring us together: team loyalties, music preference, hobbies, political ideology, style, economic status, cultural background, beach or mountains, CNN or Fox News, Paleo or good food (you know it's true), Starbucks or "keep it local, bro," Dunkin' Donuts or Tim Horton's (my Canadian friends), vegan (not me) or carnivore (me). You get the idea. We could keep going with almost anything, serious or not, and discover a multitude of subjects, ideas, and stances that divide us. How is true community even possible with so many differences?

Theologian D. A. Carson notes that

> the church is . . . made up of natural enemies. What binds us together is not common education, common race, common income levels, common politics, common nationality, common accents, common jobs, or anything else of that sort. Christians come together . . . because they have all been saved by Jesus Christ and owe him a common allegiance. . . . They are a band of natural enemies who love one another for Jesus' sake.[1]

The gospel allows people with nothing in common to find common ground in their need for a Savior. And as they begin their journey in community, they are afforded a foundation for love, care, and mutual support in spite of apparent differences.

THE END GOAL

I'm sure you have heard the phrase, *Begin with the end in mind.* My father was a carpenter. He never built a house without first knowing what the completed structure would look like. Biblical community is no different. Our goal is to build communities that together fulfill Paul's exhortation in Romans 12:1: "I appeal to you therefore, brothers, by the mercies of God, to present your bodies as a living sacrifice, holy and acceptable to God, which is your spiritual worship." The hope is that we would build communities who sacrificially worship God, who by His mercy has given us all the acceptance, worth, and identity we will ever need.

Church attendance alone will never be enough. Another class on biblical theology will not solve the problem. Sharing a building for one hour each Sunday cannot forge community for people like Damon and Gene. It takes more. Ephesians 2:18–22 tells us,

> For through him we both have access in one Spirit to the Father. So then you are no longer strangers and aliens, but you are fellow citizens with the saints and members of the household of God, built on the foundation of the apostles and prophets, Christ Jesus himself being the cornerstone, in whom the whole structure, being joined together, grows into a holy temple in the Lord. In him you also are being built together into a dwelling place for God by the Spirit.

Paul establishes that the path to God, for all people, comes through Jesus Christ. He is the only way that broken people can be made whole. And because all people are made whole through Christ, they can be built together in a unique relationship.

THE FAILED PURSUIT

Ultimately everyone shares two similar searches: significance and a salve for loneliness. Unfortunately most of humanity does so apart from Christ. According to the Pew Research Center, more than 4.7 billion people are without Christ.[2] Close to 70 percent of the world's population seek solutions in something other than Jesus.

Many search for significance through other people: just check out football fans or watch parents at their kid's spelling bee competition. Some search for significance through foolish pursuits such as food, comfort, sex, money, addictions, or careers. Although they may provide temporary satisfaction, ultimately they are impotent to address the heart's insatiable longing.

You are no different. Consider the vast array of things—other than Christ—that you have sought fulfillment in.

Evaluate yourself:

- What or who does your schedule revolve around?
- Where do you spend your disposable income?
- Where does your time go when you get to choose?
- What are you most consumed by? (Politics, sports, music, television, career, school, relationships, others' perception, money?)
- What crushes you when it fails you?
- What conversational topics do you get most excited about?
- What motivates you? When you wake up in the morning, what is on your mind?

Our affections may be different, but we all look somewhere for meaning. One of the most subtle and paradoxical of all places we look is through relationships with other people. We are lonely so surely we will find the cure by seeking genuine relationships, right? Edward Welch states, "We believe that people have the god-like ability to fill us with esteem, love, admiration, acceptance, and respect. We worship people because we perceive that they have the power to give us something."[3]

I love my wife, Renie (pronounced *rainy*, like the weather). When we were first married, I placed an unbelievable amount of pressure on her to bring me the worth and value I desperately desired. Without knowing it, I was asking her to give me what was designed for God only to supply. Renie makes for an incredible wife, but a terrible god.

Whatever or whomever you glory in (try to find significance from) will become the place you seek substance from. In due time it will assuredly fail you, and the sense of brokenness will only increase. In Psalm 16:4, David stated, "The sorrows of those who run after another god shall multiply."

Ironically we do not find significance or the cure for our loneliness in relationships with other people but in relationship with God

Himself. He alone can sustain the weight of our worship. Through shared relationship with Him, then, people can be bound to one another in a unity that transcends the very longing for relationships itself.

A BETTER WAY

When we place too many expectations on our relationships, they can easily consume us and ultimately let us down. They become bad only when we try to draw life from them. I heard one pastor say that when we take a good thing and make it a God thing, then it becomes a bad thing. Having a great wife is not a bad thing, but when I make her ultimate, I debilitate my pursuit of the end goal: the worship of God.

We all glory in something, and what we glory in, we commit to and sacrifice for. Damon does. Gene does. I do. Your great-great-grandmother did. The apostle Paul did. The pope does. And I'm guessing you do too. The fact that we are all prone to follow the deceptive path of finding meaning in created things should drive us to something more stable and lasting.

The prophet Jeremiah exposes this common search for glory:

"Has a nation ever changed its gods? (Yet they are not gods at all.) But my people have exchanged their glorious God for worthless idols. Be appalled at this, you heavens, and shudder with great horror," declares the LORD. "My people have committed two sins: They have forsaken me, the spring of living water, and have dug their own cisterns, broken cisterns that cannot hold water." (Jer. 2:11–13 NIV)

Jeremiah gives great illustrative language for our two overarching sins: (1) We have forsaken God who brings life; (2) we have turned to what is broken and brings death.

The prophet refers to God using wonderfully vivid language: God is a "spring of living water." In contrast to all other dry cisterns, including relationships, God will never run dry. He is continually fresh and capable of meeting everyone's needs.

During the summer of 2001, I traveled to Siem Reap, Cambodia, to teach English and spread the gospel among the Khmer people. Late each afternoon the mission team and I bought bottles of water from the market across the street from our inn. If you have ever traveled to a third-world country, then you've heard it repeated, "Don't drink the water." Bottled water is your best friend, while well or tap water can become your worst nightmare.

About two weeks into my time in Siem Reap, I became deathly ill. My sickness led to extreme dehydration, which is one of the worst experiences—especially when it's 100 degrees and you are more than nine thousand miles from home.

The simple cure for dehydration is water, so my fellow travelers went to the market and bought me as many bottles of water as I could handle. I drank and drank, but my health continued to decline. Finally, after a couple days, one of our leaders went back to the market and talked with the man selling the water. He discovered that the vender wasn't selling pure bottled water, but refilling old bottles with unfiltered tap water.

The water we thought was pure was actually filled with parasites. So as I drank, believing the water would heal me, in reality, it was destroying my insides. Instead of restoring life, it was leading me toward death.

Often we seek what we think will bring us life when it is actually deceptively leading us toward self-inflicted destruction. Have you experienced this? Have you seen others walk through this? Damon thought that workplace success would quench his craving and yet he was continuously thirsty for more, whereas Gene thought domination over others would satisfy, and yet it led only to more anger.

The church may even serve as a pseudo-god. We foolishly believe that if we show up each Sunday, avoid the big sins, sing the songs, and listen through the sermon, we are somehow right with God.

You've probably seen this before: a man's life is falling apart and he doesn't know where else to turn. So he runs to the church and throws himself into its ministries. But it is often short-lived. A few months later, this man who was seemingly passionate about the things of God is back to his old ways. Why? He had turned to religious performance and not to the love of God.

When you put anything in the place that belongs only to God, you fail in your pursuits before you even begin the journey.

Reality:

- The money will never be enough.
- Your daughter will not be perfect.
- Your son will disrespect you.
- The new car will lose its luster.
- The addiction will bring shame.
- Your church will let you down.
- The newness of the relationship will wear off.

The first step on the right path is to admit that we are all broken. Like Adam and Eve following their sin, we need our "eyes opened" to see our sin clearly. We can then, with eyes wide open, see our mutual need for a Savior. And this awareness sets the stage for us to be clothed by the blood sacrifice of Another, as Adam and Eve were in the garden. Genesis 3:6–7 tell us that

When the woman saw that the tree was good for food, and that it was a delight to the eyes, and that the tree was to be desired to make one wise, she took of its fruit and ate, and she also gave some to her husband who was with her, and he ate. Then the eyes of both were opened, and they knew that they were naked. And they sewed fig leaves together and made themselves loincloths.

I love how illusionist Harris III stated this battle: "The first man and woman were closer to God than any other creature on earth. They had everything they could have ever wanted: healthy timeless bodies, an endless supply of food and water, and a beautiful garden in which to live and play. Still, they reached for the mirage of more."[4]

> What we glory in is what we ultimately worship, and everything —except for Jesus— eventually crumbles under the weight of worship.

From Genesis 3 to the New Testament to the maps in the back of your Bible (okay, maybe not the maps) to today, we see the conjoined cord of sin's deception and the failed pursuits that end in dissatisfaction and shame. It is only when we seek God fully that we find true meaning. What we glory in is what we ultimately worship, and everything—except for Jesus—eventually crumbles under the weight of worship.

The universal need for a Savior, a true source of living water, gives us the correct awareness to find common ground and is foundational to forming a healthy community. Within the healthy communities I have been part of, I've found that when we recognize and acknowledge our idols (anything we put in the place of God), we are at the best starting point to engage in rich relationships that fight for and love one another deeply. We learn quickly that everyone is in a similar place and that we all need God's grace. In other words, biblical community is the best place for us to keep focused on the most important and significant relationship—with Christ—and we each encourage and challenge one another to keep healthy perspectives with everything else. As we see the

> Mercy not only redirects our individual paths, but it merges our paths together toward a unified destination.

common ground of our failed attempts toward purpose, we will need others to help point to the truth of God's sufficiency. As Paul reminds us in 2 Corinthians 12:9: God's "grace is sufficient for you, for [His] power is made perfect in weakness."

MERCY REDIRECTS OUR PATH

So how do we create communities where Jesus is worshiped above all else? What moves us beyond our differences and our sinful desires to a place of unity and adoration for Christ? What brings two distinctly different guys like Damon and Gene together in community and on mission?

Mercy.

Mercy not only redirects our individual paths, but it merges our paths together toward a unified destination. Look at Romans 12:1 again: "Therefore, I urge you, brothers and sisters, in view of God's mercy, to offer your bodies as a living sacrifice, holy and pleasing to God—this is your true and proper worship" (NIV). The beginning of verse 1 uses the word *therefore*, which acts as a bridge between two thoughts. Whenever we see *therefore*, we need to ask, "What is it there for?" In other words, what is before it, what is after it, and how do they connect?

After "therefore," Paul gives us the communal aspect of the passage as he addresses the audience as "brothers and sisters." Then Paul leads us to look at God's mercy ("in view of God's mercy"). Mercy is simply God's unrelenting compassion for us, in which He sympathetically entered our sorrow and pain (see John 1:14).

As a new believer, I often heard people quote Romans 12:1, almost always as a challenge to individual Christians. *You, as an individual, are to offer your individual body to God as an individual, living sacrifice.* But this doesn't seem to be Paul's point. He writes to the church in Rome and calls them to offer their worship and sacrifice together as brothers and sisters.

Here's where a good, Southern vocabulary helps us apply the text well. We could read: "Therefore, in light of God's mercies, y'all should offer your bodies." *You all*—that is the point. We are to *all together* offer our respective bodies to God because He has shown mercy to us all.

As a community we offer God our sacrifice, worship, and glory because of His mercy. God's mercy is the redirecting effect of our affections. Whereas Romans 12:1–13 displays how we live the Christian life with one another in community, the preceding chapters, Romans 1–11, systematically describe the *foundation* for authentic community: God's mercy. So the "therefore" connects us back to all of Romans 1–11. Pastor Danny Akin summed it up this way:

The word *therefore* is there for a reason. It is connecting us back not only to chapter 11, verses 33–36, but it is connecting back to the entirety of Romans 1–11. In fact, when Paul uses the phrase "the mercies of God," that is his shorthand way of describing all we read in Romans 1 through Romans 11."[5]

In keeping with Paul's commands, we can also use a therefore: In light of God's mercies toward us, *therefore*, we can build a foundation for change and form solid, biblical community only as we seek and see the mercy of God together.

As we read Scripture and seek to understand its implications, we must always interpret Scripture with Scripture, not with our feelings or self-deduced opinions. To help us grasp more clearly the thread of mercy that runs through the fabric of Romans 1–11 as it applies to community, let's take a quick walk back through those chapters.

UNDERSTANDING MERCY

The most incredible theologian, the apostle Paul, devoted 315 verses (Romans 1–11) to building the tension of man's sin and God's holiness, while unfolding the peace delivered through God's mercies. In Romans 1:22–23 we learn that we either glory in the Creator God or we exchange Him for created things, and in doing so we rightfully earn the judgment of a righteous God, of whose holiness we fall short (see Romans 2 and 3:23). Falling short of God's holy standard is sin, and sin emanates from it the weight of guilt and shame and the inherent response that something must be done to make things right.

For centuries, humanity has fallen into the performance trap of religion. Religion carries with it the idea of working to rise above sin, or obeying strict rules to counteract our sin, in hopes of earning our own righteousness. Paul tells us in Romans 4:4–5, however, that righteousness cannot be earned through work, but only by having faith in the One who has accomplished everything for us. The religious trap is so dangerous because it is the exact opposite of the gospel.

In Romans 5 and 6, Paul reminds us that the penalty for sin is death, but that Jesus lived the life we could not live and then died the death we deserve, while Romans 7 communicates the good news that we can be restored and made right through faith. The condemnation we once felt dissipates in contact with God's love, and the pursuit of daily holiness is possible not by our own works but through a relationship with Jesus (Rom. 8).

God took the life of Jesus so that He did not have to take ours. This is good news; this is the gospel. The Creator God of the universe based salvation on no prior merit of our own, offering salvation to those who believe by faith and faith alone (see Rom. 9 and 10). Finally, Paul arrives at the end of his extensive explanation by saying that the mercies of our holy God cannot be easily described:

Oh, the depth of the riches and wisdom and knowledge of God! How unsearchable are his judgments and how inscrutable his ways! "For who has known the mind of the Lord, or who has been his counselor? Or who has given a gift to him that he might be repaid?" For from him and through him and to him are all things. To him be the glory forever. Amen. (Rom. 11:33–36)

And then we find ourselves back at the distinctive transition of Romans 12:1: *Therefore*. Paul is urging us in light of God's mercies, which we see described in Romans 1–11, to then worship (Rom. 12:1) and live by those mercies through gospel community (Rom. 12:2–13). God's mercy redirects us back to the end goal.

THE RESULT OF MERCY

God's mercy is the basis for community. So when we look at Damon and Gene, we initially and obviously see how different they are, and going deeper we see that they are more alike than different because of their need for God's mercy. Those apart from Christ may share common ground that is fleeting and surface-level, but those in Christ have a deeper unity made possible only through God's mercy.

When Damon and Gene surrendered their lives to Jesus and began their journey of transformation, Damon did not miraculously become athletic, nor did Gene enter the University of Oxford. But they found meaning and purpose for the first time. As they came together in community, the struggles were messy. Though they gained a new heart through Jesus, learning to live out of that new identity was a constant fight.

As change in them took place, mission became a by-product of their transformation. Both began helping within our church's mission initiatives and eventually found themselves serving together in the city. Missions became a regular part of their lives, and community became the context in which they grew spiritually and served willingly.

Our tendency is to assume that people like Damon and Gene will never live in community, and yet I witnessed these two very different people walk together in deep community. God's mercy doesn't just make us acquaintances but confidants. They confessed and repented together from sin and walked in the new identity and new mission given to them through the gospel. Although Damon and Gene were as opposite as two individuals could possibly be, they discovered common ground, unity, and the mission of God.

As we seek to live in community, it is vitally important to recognize who we once were and where we came from, otherwise we will continue to ignore the possibility of community with others who seem so different from our "norm." Growth in this gospel allows us to be more welcoming to the melting pot society that we live in. Tim Keller stated, "When we believe the gospel, we receive a profound union with others who believe, even though they may be radically different than us in every other way."[6] The message of God's mercy has leveled the playing field. In his classic *Life Together*, Dietrich Bonhoeffer paints a beautiful picture of gospel unity: "Our community with one another consists solely in what Christ has done to both of us."[7]

Yes, we are saved as individuals, but it's in the common ground with others—not necessarily exactly like us—that we grow and experience God's mercies and mission.

Community begins by understanding that we all seek lesser things than God to give us life. As we worship God and God alone, however, He not only draws us to Himself, but toward unity with one another. This is the genesis of how authentic community is built. Ultimately, Dietrich Bonhoeffer concludes that community is only as strong as what it is built upon, and community built on the gospel is the only thing deep enough to make Gene and Damon not only friends, but brothers. You can't have a community without common ground, and through the gospel, we have the deepest commonality that exists: the blood of Christ that unites us as family.

GETTING PRACTICAL

- **WHAT** do you need to repent of glorying in other than Christ?
- **WHAT** broken cisterns have you drunk from, thinking they would lead you to life?
- **HOW** is your unwillingness to repent hindering your pursuit of community?
- **HOW** have you seen friendships develop with people you probably never would have been friends with outside of your common ground in the gospel?
- **IF** you don't share community with those who are different from you, what's holding you back?

"Do not be conformed to this world, but be transformed by the renewal of your mind, that by testing you may discern what is the will of God, what is good and acceptable and perfect."

—ROMANS 12:2

CHAPTER 3

CONTINUOUSLY TRANSFORMED

Are you watching your television or is your television watching you?" Neil Postman asked this startling question in *How to Watch the TV News*.[1] His point was that TV marketers constantly watch their audience in an effort to get people to buy their product or service.

Advertising pressures come at us from all directions: television, web, radio, print, signage, direct mail, texting campaigns, email, social media ads, and more.

Advertising agencies even have technology that detects where you go while on the web, how long you are there, what time of day or night you visit, and what links you most frequent from that particular page. Not only do these programs learn where you spend your time, they also generate a custom campaign distinctly for you that "magically" shows up as ads on the sites you visit at the precise times you visit them.

Why do companies pay millions of dollars to identify this information about you? *Conformity.*

They know that people who have brand loyalty tend to move in packs. The once-obscure fashion trend seemingly becomes mainstream overnight. The TV show moves from a relative unknown to a cultural phenomenon in a season.

Marketing works. Why? Because people believe the product offers some form of "good news." Consider the average sports car commercial. It is filled with beautiful people, in love with one another, celebrating the thrill of a life that cannot get any better. Oh, and by the way, this little car makes all of that possible. Love. Happiness. Excitement. All for the price of a new Lexus. This is good news indeed!

And people rush to a product when they believe it can deliver the good news it promises.

The problem is it won't—in fact, it can't—deliver on its promises. Products will always come up short.

Fortunately, we have "good news" that is far better than any marketer's promise. This good news proclaims all that God has done, and is doing, to reclaim a broken world from sin's plight. But for it to work at its strongest and most powerful, people who trust in this good news must work *together* to transform into the Christlikeness that comes through the power of God's Spirit.

OUR EXTENDED FAMILY

Perhaps the greatest biblical passage on the idea of community is in Ephesians. After scaling the heights of the majesty of God's work to save fallen sinners, Paul wrote,

> There is one body and one Spirit—just as you were called to the one hope that belongs to your call—one Lord, one faith, one baptism, one God and Father of all, who is over all and through all and in all. But grace was given to each one of us according to the measure of Christ's gift. (Eph. 4:4–7)

Such language was surely astounding to the early church. Until this point in redemptive history, the Jewish nation had unique access to God. They were His people and He was their God. In spite of their treacherous ways, God had delivered them from slavery, given them

His law, and allowed them to worship Him through the sacrificial system.

But Paul showed us that through Christ's work, all people—not just Jews—could be made right with God. Through faith, people of all ethnicities could call God their Father. These people are united, according to Paul, in one body. Why? Because there is one Lord, one faith, one baptism. *Since there is only one God, there is only one people of God.* This one people of God is now united as a family with God Himself as their Father. The church then is one really big, really diverse family.

My friend Matt is an only child and is fairly reserved. His wife, Sarah, on the other hand, thrives in big groups. When Matt's family sat for a meal, everyone could hear the forks clanging on the plates as each person struggled to find something to talk about. Sarah's family meals, on the other hand, were sheer chaos with people sitting everywhere and kids running around like at a neighborhood playground.

The first time Matt and Sarah shared a holiday meal with her extended family, Matt sat in stunned apprehension. "All of these people are related to you?" he asked.

Yes, they were. And once Matt and Sarah were married, they were related to him as well. He went from a small family to a large family, and by virtue of his marriage, had to learn to love these new family members.

God's family works this way. He saves people from all walks and places them, together, in His church. They look different, talk different, and come from a host of different backgrounds. But once they become Christians, they are all part of the family.

A GOOD NEWS FAMILY

In one sense all of humanity is part of the same family. As we saw in chapter 2, all people share something in common: sin. Sure, our sins may be different, but at the core all people have a propensity to rebel against God. We all share some bad news in common.

By virtue of Christ's saving work, however, we share in the good news. In the ancient near East it was common for a herald to run back into town following a military battle to declare the victory. Everyone would celebrate and the spoils of victory would be spread to the people.

In the same fashion, the Bible proclaims: "Jesus has won the victory. He has defeated Satan, sin, and death. You can be saved!" All those who trust in this work share in the spoils of the victory. They are united in this good news. Just as people unite around the good news that a Lexus commercial promises, the church unites around the good news that Jesus promises. And He can actually deliver on His promises.

PEER PRESSURE IS A GOOD THING

As a child you probably heard that peer pressure was bad. "If Susie jumps off a bridge, would you do it too?" our frustrated parents asked us. The answer was seemingly clear: no! No one would be so foolish as to jump off a bridge simply because her friend did. Our parents understood how strong our tendency is to conform to other people.

But peer pressure can be a good thing. The same tendencies that prompt people to follow one another into ever-increasing forms of idolatry can also strengthen people toward Christlikeness. And because the gospel is far greater news than sin's lies, we find greater victory when we work together than when we try to go it alone.

> To conform is to be shaped by external pressure, whereas transformation is a radical altering from the inside out.

Consider Paul's words: "Do not be conformed to this world, but be transformed by the renewal of your mind, that by testing you may discern what is the will of God, what is good and acceptable and perfect" (Romans 12:2). Paul is not writing to isolated individuals but to the church. His point is clear: the church can walk together in the process of transformation.

To conform is to be shaped by external pressure, whereas transformation is a radical altering from the inside out. The Greek word used for "be transformed" is *metamorphoō*. Our English word *metamorphosis* is derived from this word, which denotes an inside-out process of change. You may remember back in science class when you learned the life cycle of our little green friend, the frog. Egg to tadpole; tadpole to tadpole with legs; tadpole with legs to young frog; young frog to bullfrog. This is the drastic transformation—metamorphosis—that takes place biologically in a frog's life. It is also the type of process that should happen within the church.

It is helpful to understand that the word *transformed* in Romans 12:2 is both in the passive voice as well as the present tense. Namely, the transformation both *has happened* and *is happening* through the Holy Spirit's power. It is a continual process. We experience a moment of instantaneous transformation (salvation), but then we continue an ongoing transforming that is the Christian life (sanctification).

Living out our faith was never intended to be done in isolation, but within a community. The gospel is the driving force to our transformation, and community is the context where the greatest growth and revolution takes place.

YOUR GREAT ENEMY

You are your own greatest enemy in this transformation process.

This past New Year's Day, my wife and I took both of our kids, five-year-old Jack and three-year-old Piper, out for doughnuts (I couldn't even last twenty-four hours on my I'm-going-to-get-healthy resolution). My wife suggested that instead of resolutions, we should each pick a word we could carry as a theme throughout the year.

My wife's word was *thankfulness*. I went with *consistent*. (I lose and gain the same twenty pounds every year.) Jack chose the word *read*, since he really wants to learn to read this year. Then we looked at Piper, who had half the chocolate glazed donut smeared on her face.

"What's your word for the year, Piper?" Renie asked.

Piper confidently announced, "My word is *me*. This is the year of *me*."

If we're honest, that's the word most of us choose. We want to make

> Distance from Christian community is a sure sign of distance from Jesus Himself.

the year and everything in it about *me*. Our culture teaches us to look out first and foremost for ourselves, before thinking of or turning to the needs or perspectives of others. We live in a culture where being self-centered is not something to turn from but something to pursue.

Individualism will often cause you and me to remove ourselves from our Christian family. The results are tragic. Consider the implications of a toddler saying, "You know, Mom and Dad, I'm glad you had me, but I think I'll go it alone. I can eat solid foods now and even make it to the potty (most of the time). I'm thankful for all you've done for me, but if you could just give me twenty dollars and take me downtown, I'll handle it from there."

The kid wouldn't make it an hour. Yet this story plays out week after week in the average church. People profess saving faith in Jesus and are baptized. Within a few months, however, they are not around the church family much anymore. They claim they have a busy work schedule or are part of a traveling sports league. Then they stop showing up, stop taking phone calls, stop going out to dinner with their church friends. They disappear for good. Twelve years of pastoral ministry has taught me that distance from Christian community is a sure sign of distance from Jesus Himself.

"It's just me and Jesus" is far from the truth of the Scriptures. Yes, Jesus saves individuals (see Eph. 2:1–10) but then He places them in the church (see Eph. 2:11–22). The notion of an individual Christian would strike the biblical authors as foolishness akin to a toddler without a family. The results of isolation are as predictable as that same toddler trying to make it alone downtown with twenty dollars. An infant Christian is no match for this world without the help of God's family, the church. Going at it alone is not the path for a disciple of Jesus. Through grace we don't just belong to Christ—we also belong to one another.

The church should function like a good family. Just as parents will teach the toddler to avoid things that will harm him, pursue things that will help him mature, and ultimately learn meaningful mission as an adult, so the church community will help teach "toddler" Christians. Over time, the church can help us be transformed from sin, lead us into the things that will cause us to grow, and mature us to live on mission with God.

TRANSFORMED FROM SIN

Our good-news family will continually battle the temptations and lure of sin. It would be nice if all desire for sin ceased the moment we were saved, wouldn't it? But it doesn't.

In chapter 2 we learned how Damon and Gene were changed after experiencing God's mercy. And though that mercy made them new (see 2 Cor. 5:17), the battle of turning from their former behaviors continues. They've had to learn what the author of Hebrews warns us about:

Take care, brothers, lest there be in any of you an evil, unbelieving heart, leading you to fall away from the living God. But exhort one another every day, as long as it is called "today," that none of you may be hardened by the deceitfulness of sin. (Hebrews 3:12–13)

He warns them as a parent warns a child. "Son, watch out when your ball rolls out into the road," a parent might say. "A car might be coming up the road that would hurt you badly." The author of Hebrews does the same thing: "Watch out. There are pressures coming that could harm or even kill you. Be on your guard."

The church is his answer to a Christian's sin problem: "Exhort one another every day." The church serves as an echo chamber for the warning: "Watch out for sin!"

This is not the only message, however. As we saw in the last chapter, it is also to remember God's mercies. Those mercies provide the basis for our minds' renewal and transformation.

The logic goes like this. The world is hostile to God and people are prone to follow one another into waywardness. Left unhindered, people will conform themselves to death, like a flock following a single sheep off a cliff. But God acts. He rescues. People are protected from conforming to the world as they call these truths to mind.

Veronica was a young lady in the church I pastored. She had a tough life growing up and got herself into a lot of trouble. Her sin and her background led her to mistrust other people, especially professing Christians who, in her mind, were judgmental of her lifestyle. She became a hermit, thinking that other people would surely criticize and condemn her.

Some people in our church befriended her. As she became more comfortable with those relationships, Veronica began attending church. Though she was fearful that she would experience the same rejection and pain she had felt from others, she allowed Christians to invite her into their homes and their lives.

> Transformation is not only from something but also to something.

Her father's death reopened old wounds. Although Veronica was scared, she explained the pain of her past to a group of women in our church, which began the healing process. That night that group helped carry the burden that had sat solely on Veronica's shoulders for most of her life. Her tears became their tears. Through those people loving and challenging her, Veronica began to move from despising community to embracing it.

Veronica's story is a perfect example of the transformation that takes place when we are part of the good-news family. Here we confidently say to one another:

- God can forgive you of any sin!
- God can protect you from any sin!
- God can love you in spite of your sin!

We must be careful as we walk with others in their sin, however. It is easy to think that we would never fall prey to the sins we see in those we are working to love. Yet in Romans 12:3 Paul reminds us that we should not "think of [ourselves] more highly than [we] ought to think, but to think with sober judgment." In other words, don't get overly excited about yourself. "But for the grace of God, so go I" is the anthem of those who know God as Father. Our community works to repeat that truth to one another.

TRANSFORMED TO HOLINESS

Transformation is not only from something but also to something. We move from sin to holiness. The word *holy* was used in the Bible to describe something that God set apart for special service. For example, the tables and tools in God's temple were holy: they were set apart for special use. The same is true for God's people. They are set apart, by virtue of their salvation, for special use. The church is God's gift to us through this transformation process:

> Let us consider how to stir up one another to love and good works, not neglecting to meet together, as is the habit of some, but encouraging one another, and all the more as you see the Day drawing near. (Heb. 10:24–25)

This is the classic "you better go to church" verse that pastors use to prompt people to be at the church building every time the doors are open. The author's point, however, is not primarily negative. He does not write, "You better go to church or really bad things will happen to you." Rather, he provides a positive rationale for being a meaningful part of the church: to stir one another to love and good deeds as we, together, await the return of Jesus Christ. Christians are to work together to fan our faith into a raging wildfire.

Consider Dan. The thought of a personal relationship with God was foreign to him. This all changed when during his college senior year he attended a Campus Crusade event with some guys from his dorm. That night he heard the gospel, confessed his sin, and was saved. Dan began to attend Crusade, where he met and dated Claire. They married within months of graduation.

Dan was a young Christian and it showed. The marriage got off to a rocky start, with Dan's selfishness exposed at every turn. Every day after work he played video games. He did nothing to love and serve his wife. And Claire was growing bitter.

What is the church's role with someone like Dan? According to Hebrews, they are to lovingly pursue him, address the selfishness they observe, remind him of his need for Christlikeness, and walk with him to change. They can share Scripture that reminds Dan of his mission to love his wife as Christ loved the church (see Eph. 5:22–33). They can provide practical advice on how they love their wives sacrificially. They can pray for Dan and send him text messages verbalizing their prayers.

Simply leaving Dan alone to wreck his marriage demonstrates a misunderstanding of the gospel. We are the church and we work *together* to pursue holiness.

TRANSFORMED TO MISSION

Finally, the church is to be a community transformed to mission. Jesus demonstrated this value when He prayed, "I do not ask for these only, but also for those who will believe in me through their word, that they may all be one, just as you, Father, are in me, and I in you, that they also may be in us, so that the world may believe that you have sent me" (John 17:20–21).

This request, which Jesus made shortly before His crucifixion, connects community, transformation, and mission. Jesus prayed that the oneness within the Trinity would be the same type of unity among the church. The outcome of this unity would then be mission—for the world to believe that Jesus is the Son of God.

Wonderfully enough, as people live together on mission, they also continually transform. Too often we think that we must first get our act together and then we can live on mission for God. Mission, however, is a perfect tool for change. If you struggle with your prayer life, love a person far from God and see if that does not prompt you to pray more consistently. If you struggle to read the Bible, serve your Muslim neighbor and dialogue about how you each understand God. If you struggle with secret sin, invite a lost friend to model their life after yours. Mission in community will expedite your personal transformation.

A COMMUNITY OF TRANSFORMATION

Transformation makes the church come alive. People no longer attend church simply to fulfill their weekly religious obligation. Instead they "do nothing from selfish ambition or conceit, but in humility count others more significant than [themselves]. Let each of you look not only to his own interests, but also to the interests of others" (Phil. 2:3–5). Imagine a church that:

- is filled with people who care more about others than they care about themselves.
- does not ask "What's in it for me?" but rather "How can I serve?"
- is a safe place to confess sin and pursue holiness.
- lives on mission to see others brought into this glorious family.

"The gospel is not palatable," notes David Platt, "but it is powerful."[2] It is powerful enough to save a hell-bent sinner from himself and from God's wrath. It is also powerful enough to place isolated individuals into a large extended family. And it is powerful enough to use this family to bring the type of transformation for which we long.

GETTING PRACTICAL

- **HOW** do you speak about the church? In what ways does this expose what you truly believe?
- **IN** what ways do you respond to sin in the church? How does this expose what you truly believe?
- **DO** you help others in their transformation process? In what ways? How does this expose what you truly believe?
- **HOW** do you partner with others to live on mission? In what ways does this expose what you truly believe?

Life in Community

THE VALUES FOR LIVING IN COMMUNITY

"For as in one body we have many members, and the members do not all have the same function, so we, though many, are one body in Christ, and individually members one of another."

—ROMANS 12:4-5

CHAPTER 4

YOUR BEST
AT THE TABLE

Churches do not always create community. At times they can do the opposite. They can function like social clubs where paid professionals provide religious services to their consumers. I, for one, have been guilty of treating the church this way. But the church is not a club to pay dues to; it's a body to belong to.

What does it look like for us to move from club to community—from a buffet table where we each grab our own wants to a family-style community table where we all bring our best to share?

THE ANATOMY OF COMMUNITY

While I was growing up I loved playing football. I wasn't the greatest player, but I practiced hard and was naïve to my weaknesses. I rarely suffered from injuries and never thought much about anything bad happening. At seventeen, that attitude isn't much of a problem. A decade later, though, that mentality can be destructive.

I know. I had reconstructive knee surgery when I was twenty-nine because I blew out my knee playing flag football. I thought I could still do everything I'd done in high school.

About a year after that surgery on my right knee, I started to play sports again. But soon I noticed that my left hamstring and calf kept cramping. I did everything I could to prevent the pain in my healthy leg. I stretched, I applied menthol gel, I wore a wrap. Yet nothing made the tightness and pain subside.

Finally after several months, I made an appointment with my orthopedic surgeon to see why my healthy leg was in such pain and what we could do about it. I had some initial ideas, but since WebMD and Wikipedia will take me only so far, I wanted a professional, medical opinion.

After the doctor examined me, he said that my left leg was being strong because my right leg was still recovering and was weak. The left leg was taking on an abnormal load and straining the muscles and ligaments as a result of my right leg muscles' atrophy. In other words, the body helps the body.

I learned a valuable lesson that day about the way the body is intended to function. When one part is weak, another part steps up to carry the weight. When one part does not work properly, another stronger part does the work for it.

> The church is not a club to pay dues to; it's a body to belong to.

It is the same functioning design for the church. Paul wrote, "As in one body we have many members, and the members do not all have the same function, so we, though many, are one body in Christ, and individually members one of another" (Rom. 12:4–5).

In 1 Thessalonians 5:14, Paul got more specific in how the church works together: "We urge you, brothers, admonish the idle, encourage the fainthearted, help the weak, be patient with them all." The church community is meant to play an active role with weaker brothers and sisters. Paul's use of the word *weak* does not mean that there is some unique category of Christians who are the weak ones and another group who are strong—like the JV and varsity team at your local high school. The reality, however, is that at some point we are all the weaker brother or sister. The church is God's gift of grace to support us in these times of weakness.

Using the body as the primary illustration for biblical community is not a stretch by any means. Throughout the New Testament we can find at least forty verses that are dedicated to displaying this picture:

- John 2:19–22
- 1 Corinthians 10:16–17
- 1 Corinthians 12:12–31
- Ephesians 1:22–23
- Ephesians 4:4
- Ephesians 4:11–16
- Ephesians 5:23
- Ephesians 5:29–30
- Colossians 1:18
- Colossians 1:24
- Colossians 2:19
- Colossians 3:15

In 1 Corinthians 12:12–27, Paul provides the most vivid picture of how the church functions as a body:

Just as the body is one and has many members, and all the members of the body, though many, are one body, so it is with Christ. For in one Spirit we were all baptized into one body—Jews or Greeks, slaves or free—and all were made to drink of one Spirit.

For the body does not consist of one member but of many. If the foot should say, "Because I am not a hand, I do not belong to the body," that would not make it any less a part of the body. And if the ear should say, "Because I am not an eye, I do not belong to the body," that would not make it any less a part of the body. If the whole body were an eye, where would be the sense of hearing? If the whole body were an ear, where would be the sense of smell? But as it is, God arranged the members in the body, each one of them, as he chose. If all were a single member, where would the body be? As it is, there are many parts, yet one body. The eye cannot say to the hand, "I have no need of you," nor again the head to the feet, "I have no need of you." On the contrary, the parts of the body that seem to be weaker are indispensable, and on those parts of the body that we think less honorable we bestow the greater honor, and our unpresentable parts are treated with greater modesty, which our more presentable parts do not require. But God has so composed the body, giving greater honor to the part that lacked it, that there may be no division in the body, but that the members may have the same care for one another. If one member suffers, all suffer together; if one member is honored, all rejoice together.

Now you are the body of Christ and individually members of it.

Although this illustration may be familiar, applying this principle is often deceptively difficult for many.

When our family moved to Atlanta, we needed to find a new church home. The process took much longer than we wanted. As we attended different services each Sunday, we didn't connect with anyone beyond "Welcome to Grace Journey Fellowship Church!" (Okay, that wasn't the name, but it's close to a lot of church names.) These churches may have had rich community, but we knew that it would take more than attending the Sunday morning service to find out. We would have to immerse ourselves in the church's day-to-day life to see how the body interacted and loved one another.

> We will not truly experience the beauty of being the body by reducing biblical community to a church gathering on Sundays.

The human body doesn't function separately six days a week and then come together on Sunday to see how the other parts did all week. The body is meant to be constantly connected, working together to achieve optimal performance. I love what C. S. Lewis says about this concept: "Christianity thinks of human individuals not as mere members of a group or items in a list, but as organs in a body—different from one another and each contributing what no other could."[1]

We will not truly experience the beauty of being the body by reducing biblical community to a church gathering on Sundays. One of the major values of biblical community is that we are always the body. What happens on Sunday mornings inside the brick and mortar of a church building is only one of its many functions. These types of gatherings are where the body celebrates all that God has done in and through them, and is then equipped to go out as the body to do the work of ministry (see Eph. 4:12). As Paul suggests, when one part of the body hurts, we hurt with it. Likewise, when part of the body has victory, we share in the win. The church is the body when it gathers in worship and when it scatters in mission.

COMMUNITY IS MORE THAN A SUNDAY

Don had been struggling with a drug addiction for years when he became part of the church I was pastoring. He was a brilliant man who held numerous degrees from esteemed universities, but lost everything when he began to use drugs. Along with that addiction came a number of other sins that slowly wrecked his life.

Hunter, one of our leaders, met and befriended Don and brought him around our community. In due time, Don plugged in and connected with other men in our church.

Don was not sober when he became part of our church. Through his addiction and the domino effect it had into all areas of life, Don carried a lot of baggage. And with that baggage came a lot of struggle and deep-rooted pain.

The easy route would have been for the community to give Don a gentle pat on the back and say, "I'll pray for you." Frequently in some church cultures that phrase unfortunately means, *Good luck with that.*

These men not only prayed for Don—they carried the burden with him. The phrase *I hurt for you* was a reality for them. They faithfully helped Don apply the gospel to his self-inflicted wounds and to the scars caused by others.

The goal was not to change Don's morals, but to continually point him to Jesus and watch Jesus heal and transform him—because moralistic actions do not transform a heart; a transformed heart leads to a change in moral action.

These men were not serving Don from a place of abundance but rather through sacrifice. When the body ministers to the body, it will always cost something. Living out gospel-centered community is not convenient. These men had families and full-time jobs, yet they would call Don daily, share meals with him regularly, have him into their homes weekly, encourage him constantly, and lovingly confront him when necessary. This was not a Sunday activity that took place for an hour and ended with a prayer and a song. Community is more than a Sunday.

God healed Don and He used His church to do it. One Sunday, after Don had been clean for seven weeks, he told me, "I would have used [drugs] more than a few times if it hadn't been for my brothers." He was able to get off drugs and stay off because of the body of Christ's glorious work. The following week, these men threw a party as Don celebrated two months of sobriety. The joy in that place was worth every ounce of sacrifice.

When the body hurts, we hurt with it. When one part celebrates, the whole body celebrates! Being the body is not about convenience but rather commitment.

BRING YOUR BEST

I like to eat. I travel a lot for my work, so I get to eat out regularly. As much as possible, I frequent local dives rather than franchises. But no matter the restaurant, the chef, the city, or the ambiance, nothing replaces a good covered-dish meal.

In the church culture I grew up in, periodically after the Sunday worship service, everyone would make their way to the fellowship hall, pull out their food dishes, and we would feast.

Each person had his or her specialty. Mrs. Polly cooked macaroni and cheese, while Mrs. Smith baked pecan pie with the pecans she'd picked and cracked from her own yard. Mr. Thompson made home-made vanilla-bean ice cream (that topped off the pie) better than any ice cream parlor you have been to.

We had sugar-cured ham with a drizzle of honey, green-bean casserole, peach cobbler, fried okra, mini ham sandwiches on poppy-seed sweet rolls, buttermilk fried chicken, and every other assortment of mouth-watering food you can imagine.

The key to this covered-dish dinner is that everyone knew what they made well, spent time putting their contribution together, and brought to the table the best they had to offer. No one tried to make better fried okra than Mrs. White. They brought their own specialty.

The covered-dish feast is an important illustration in the life of the church. God has given each of us our own specialty that He specifically designed us to have and use. That includes you.

The greatest meals are the ones where everyone brings their best. The table is not a table for one. It's an enormous banquet table where God Himself invites all to come and dine. Your "covered dish" is the particular gifts God has given you, no matter what they may be. Paul tells us that since we have "gifts that differ according to the grace given to us, let us use them: if prophecy, in proportion to our faith; if service, in our serving; the one who teaches, in his teaching; the one who exhorts, in his exhortation; the one who contributes, in generosity; the one who leads, with zeal; the one who does acts of mercy, with cheerfulness" (Rom. 12:6–8).

Your gifts were not designed to be used in seclusion, but to be used to serve and bless the community. Without fail, any place in Scripture where you see the "gifts" listed, they are always mentioned within the context of biblical community—to edify those who congregate at the table. For instance, 1 Peter 4:10 says, "Based on the gift each one has received, use it to serve others, as good managers of the varied grace of God" (HCSB).

When we consider the types of gifts God gives, we can look at three primary places—Romans 12, Ephesians 4, and 1 Corinthians 12—to find more specifics. These lists reveal the brilliant way in which God has assembled His body.

ROMANS 12	1 CORINTHIANS 12
Exhortation	Administration
Giving	Apostolic
Leadership	Discernment
Mercy	Faith
Prophecy	Healing
Service	Helps
Teaching	Knowledge
	Miracles
EPHESIANS 4	Prophecy
	Teaching
Apostle	Speaking in tongues
Evangelist	Interpretation of tongues
Pastor	Wisdom
Prophet	
Teacher	

What an astounding list! Knowing the importance God places on your gifts within His kingdom, you can apply them with zeal.

ZOE MEANS LIFE

This past year, I received an earth-shaking text message from my best friend, who now leads the church that we planted and pastored together for seven years. He and his wife had just discovered that their three-year-old daughter, Zoe, had stage-4 cancer. What started for them as a fun day at the zoo ended in a hospital room with grave news.

They'd named their little girl Zoe because in Greek *zoe* means *life.* Now this little girl, who was once full of life, was poisoned by cancer.

Renie and I were heartbroken, especially since we lived more than three hours from them. Immediately we got our kids out of bed, packed our bags, and headed for our friends' home. Although we could stay only a few days, we wanted to be with them as much as we could.

During the drive, we called others who were part of their community and talked through how we could all love this family in the best way possible. We were amazed to discover that we were already late to the game. People wanted to serve any way they could. For some it was organizing and administrating, for others it was encouragement, while some wanted to give generously.

One family had taken our friends' other daughter for the night. Another had created an online calendar to organize meal service to them. Some were scheduling times for people to pray together, while some groups were already gathering. Others had taken over mowing duties.

Since one of my gifts is leadership, I listened and then led in the places that still needed help. One friend mentioned that the medical bills would begin to pile up and wondered if we all could do something financially to help. So I called a lunch meeting to brainstorm the opportunities.

The next day a banker, a website developer, a graphic artist, a writer, a video producer, and I gathered for lunch and talked about how collectively we could assist. None of us was wealthy by any stretch, but we knew we had to do something.

Within forty-eight hours of that lunch meeting, the group created and produced a website and a video that told the story of this amazing family and their little girl Zoe. Within a few weeks, people from all over the world learned of Zoe and donated more than $75,000 to the family's needs. It was awe-inspiring to watch as each person who made up this community offered what they knew they could bring.

Driving back to Atlanta was tough, but we experienced peace knowing that we left behind a community who were applying God's grace to one another through their spiritual gifts.

While Zoe continues to battle cancer, she is not doing it alone. The community around her is strong. Zoe means life, and that is exactly what her story and community are portraying. Through Zoe's life we have been given a picture of the body functioning as the body should.

COMMUNITY IS THE DEFINITIVE TEST

If you have been around the church for any time, you have heard about (or even taken) a spiritual gifts test. Basically you answer a series of questions about yourself. Those answers are inserted into a formula that then draws a score or ranking for the spiritual gifts listed in Romans 12, Ephesians 4, and/or 1 Corinthians 12. The results usually announce your top three spiritual gifts.

This type of test is a great tool and I recommend using one.[2] A lot of these tests present exceptional descriptions and distinctive natures of each gift. But as the creators will attest, the tests are only a tool and not a definite conclusion. The best tool for discerning your spiritual gifts is not a test, but the body of Christ. There you will find out what you bring to the table. Ask others to speak into your life and be willing to listen to their insight. Ask them to observe where they see God using you most significantly.

Renie had taken one spiritual gifts test after another but never felt as though the results made a lot of sense. Her highest score was always on the gift of mercy, but she didn't feel as if that were her gift. My wife is awesome and is super nice, but I've been injured enough (bad knee) to know that the mercy thing isn't that high on her abilities scale either. Renie is a registered nurse. Her job required her to have a good bedside manner and to show mercy as she gave medical attention to her patients, so of course the test results were skewed because of her profession.

It wasn't until we were walking deep in community with others that she began to grasp the gifts God had given her. It took time and people who cared enough to point out to her where they saw her gifts appearing.

The goal is not to get you to do everything, but to get everyone to do something.

Renie is extremely discerning. She has the ability to see through the minutia and find the truth regarding people. Not only was this a blessing to her but it was also a blessing to our community. She was instrumental in helping us make decisions regarding some of our leadership and who should serve where within our church. When we were considering a couple people to elevate to new areas of responsibility, Renie pointed out some things that we had never really observed. What should have been clear to us were land mines that she was able to uncover, and as a result saved our community a lot of heartache and frustration. It was through community that my wife discovered her gifts, and it was in community that she put them into action.

Through the voice of community God will speak loudly of the gifts He has given you. Allow your group to help point you toward what you bring to the table and direct them to what they bring as well. The goal is not to get you to do everything, but to get everyone to do something.

What is your something? As you discover the grace gift that God has given you, understand that it is only beneficial as you apply it within the community and the mission context God has given you. Bring your best to the table so that all who dine can enjoy.

MISSION THREAD

When the church *becomes* the body, then we also experience mission. As Paul concludes his illustration, he furnishes the key to the entire notion: "Now you are the body of Christ and individually members of it" (1 Cor. 12:27). This is not just any body, this is the body of Christ exhibited for the world to see and be invited into. We get to put Jesus on display as the body ministers to the body. It is attractive and compelling when the church operates with the mantra: everyone plays a role and everyone should bring their best.

GETTING PRACTICAL

- **WHAT** spiritual gifts or passions do you think you have been given?
- **HAVE** those gifts been affirmed by your community? If so, in what ways? If not, who could you ask to confirm them?
- **IN** what ways are you using those gifts within the church?
- **HOW** can you more effectively use the gifts God has given you to serve others?

"Let love be genuine. . . ."

—ROMANS 12:9

CHAPTER 5

NO MASKS ALLOWED

N o one knows when the process starts. It may begin long before we are ever consciously aware of it. But its presence is exceedingly clear once someone enters their teenage years.

"How are you doing, sweetheart?" a mom might ask her middle-school daughter.

"Fine," she spits out, accompanied by a disgusted scowl.

Even a naïve mom knows the truth: her daughter's answer does not match the reality of her heart. She says "fine" because she is either unable or unwilling to share her true feelings.

Adults, it seems, have mastered this art. Imagine a group of middle-aged businessmen sharing an evening meal. They talk readily about the official's blown call in the previous night's game, the latest scandal surrounding a reputable politician, or the potential business deal that hinges on

Honesty is one of the greatest means of fostering genuine biblical community.

the success of the next day's meeting. But if you want the conversation to screech to a halt, ask: "So, bro, how are you doing?"

"Well . . . um . . . I'm okay. . . . Things at home are . . . well . . .

they're fine. . . . The kids . . . I guess . . . well, it's just life, you know?
But I guess . . . well . . . I'm fine!"

"Fine" is the universal non-answer.

The church is often no different. Recently, a friend told me about a
man in his late sixties who joined a small group for the first time. Part
of the group's experience was to ask each person, "How was your walk
with Jesus this week?"

When it was this man's turn to answer, he replied, "I've got to be
honest with you. I've been in church for more than forty years and no
one has ever asked me that question. I don't know what to say."

All he'd ever known to do was casually shake hands with those worshiping, and if asked how he was doing, reply, "I'm fine."

This man's candor is insightful and convicting. The church may be
filled with eloquent sermons, uplifting music, and diverse programs,
without actually talking about the state of our hearts. Yet honesty is
one of the greatest means of fostering genuine biblical community.

A SIN AS OLD AS THE GARDEN

Our propensity for giving superficial or downright false responses
began at the dawn of creation. Humankind, fashioned at the climax of
God's created work, was given astounding provision. Adam had meaningful work as he developed the latent potential of the good world.
He had a glorious helpmate—a wife God presented as a grace-gift to
partner with him in their mission. Finally, and most important, he
could have a deep relationship with God Himself.

His one prohibition was to refrain from eating from the Tree of
Knowledge of Good and Evil. Simple enough, right? He had every
other tree from which to eat. In fact he had everything that he could
ever need or want. But he ate from *that* tree.

You may be familiar with the results. God condemned Adam's dis-
obedience and doled out consequences that applied to the man, the
woman, the serpent, and the world itself (see Gen. 3:14–19). These
consequences may also have included what happened before the curses
came:

The eyes of both were opened, and they knew that they were naked. And they sewed fig leaves together and made themselves loincloths.

And they heard the sound of the LORD God walking in the garden in the cool of the day, and the man and his wife hid themselves from the presence of the LORD God among the trees of the garden. But the LORD God called to the man and said to him, "Where are you?" And he said, "I heard the sound of you in the garden, and I was afraid, because I was naked, and I hid myself." He said, "Who told you that you were naked? Have you eaten of the tree of which I commanded you not to eat?" The man said, "The woman whom you gave to be with me, she gave me fruit of the tree, and I ate." Then the LORD God said to the woman, "What is this that you have done?" The woman said, "The serpent deceived me, and I ate." (Genesis 3:7–13)

The man and the woman did three things. First, they tried to cover themselves. They obviously felt ashamed, recognized their nakedness, and tried to mask their embarrassment. Second, they hid. Has there ever been a more comical scene than a couple trying to hide behind a bush from an omniscient God? Third, they blamed. The finger-pointing moved from the woman to the snake, demonstrating that they were unwilling to bear the responsibility for their actions.

Shame, hiding, and blame—the response of the first couple and of all humanity to sin. We, likewise, try to hide from our sin and pretend that it did not happen or that God will not know. We try to blame something else—from other people, to our past, to inanimate objects—for our sinful ways. We cower in shame, knowing that we are guilty, and looking for something, anything, to make us look better.

Dwayne was a well-respected leader in his business, his community, his church, and his family. What each of these groups didn't know was that Dwayne had a secret life, which consisted of late nights out carousing, getting drunk, and sleeping around. Once, when confronted in a lie, he sought to mask his sinfulness by following Adam's path. First, he felt shame so he attempted to cover for his sin with a host of good deeds—everything from serving as a church deacon, to chairing the neighborhood watch committee, to volunteering to coach his child's Little League team. He hoped that these good deeds would somehow make up for his failures. Second, he tried to hide. He increasingly isolated himself, hoping to avoid having to confront the truth. Finally, he looked for someone to blame. His dad was an alcoholic, his career was stressful, and his wife didn't seem to desire him anymore. Surely he was justified in his actions. His continual sin leads him to also become a hypocrite. Dwayne's story uncovers a reality that we know all too well.

COMING CLEAN IN COMMUNITY

In Romans 12, Paul provides practical advice on how to move beyond that hypocritical side. We have already seen that he challenges us to corporately offer ourselves as a living sacrifice before a holy God. This then allows us to avoid conformity to the world and instead pursue transformation. Paul then writes, "Let your love be genuine."

The Greek word for "genuine" in Romans 12:9 is *anypokritos*, from which our English word *hypocrite* is derived. This word was used in the ancient theater where actors did not have the luxury of Hollywood production standards. When seeking to change characters or portray a differing emotion, they would wear a mask, which would transform them into the character they wanted to convey to the audience.

Paul knows that we Christians are tempted to do the same thing. We put on masks rather than be authentic with one another. As a result, Paul challenges us to scorn hypocrisy and choose genuineness, which is the opposite of hypocrisy.

In the NIV translation, Paul writes, "Love must be sincere." The word *sincere* is derived from the Latin word *sine* (without) and *cera* (wax). According to folk history, merchants who sold cheap pottery would fill in the imperfections and cracks with wax in order to give the appearance that the piece was worth more than it actually was. When holding this pottery up to light, a person could easily observe the cover-up, because the light would shine through the areas where the wax had been placed, revealing the cracks. Authentic, quality pieces were often stamped with the phrase *sine cera* or "without wax." Christians are to live without wax, genuine and sincere in our actions toward one another.

Recently I traveled to Oklahoma City. When I went to pick up my rental car at the airport, I learned that they were out of cars—including the one I had reserved. All they had left was a Ford F150 truck, which I got for the same price as my car.

Moments later I was driving through the Stock Yards of Oklahoma City with the windows down, a toothpick in my mouth, and country music blaring. I was even tempted to stop in a store called Langston's and buy a pair of boots and a cowboy hat. As I drove along, I'd nod my head at the local cowboys and they'd nod back, as I owned the road in my newfound identity.

That day I put on the act of being a country music cowboy, but the truth is I was wearing straight-leg jeans, a hoodie, and a pair of Vans. I would have fit much better in a Toyota Yaris. Plus I have a deep disdain for country music. I didn't want anyone to know I was wearing skate shoes or that I preferred a band called Mutemath, who is as far from country as you can get.

If we're honest, we all put on masks to become something we are not. Unfortunately, Sundays and Wednesdays (or whenever the church gathers) have become a stereotypical occasion for putting on your best mask. I can think of numerous Sundays when I've looked at my kids and said, "Get over it, quit crying, and put a smile on your face." Even worse, I can't count the number of times that Renie and I have plastered on smiles when we felt like crying.

THE ENEMY OF HONESTY

Why do we consistently choose hypocrisy over honesty? I think the answer is simple: fear.

The story is often repeated of a young lawyer who had just started his own law firm. He leased a small storefront and took out a loan for some pristine office furniture. Although he had not landed his first client, he sat faithfully in his office. Finally, someone walked through the front door. The lawyer immediately began a frantic rush to appear busy and important. He picked up the phone and began rattling off a bunch of legal rhetoric, as if there were another person on the other end of the line. After making the man wait a few minutes, the lawyer hung up the phone and said to the waiting man, "What can I help you with?"

"I'm just here to set up your phone line."[1]

That story displays an immaturity and foolishness on the young lawyer's part. He was afraid of someone thinking of—and judging— him as a failure.

Fear cripples our community as well. We are ashamed by our inability to do what we know is right. We wrongly think that God will condemn us if we own our sin before Him. We forget that "there is therefore now no condemnation for those who are in Christ Jesus" (Rom. 8:1).

We also think that people will condemn us. We fear their judgmental glances, gossip, or accusations. Without a clear grasp of honesty's power, we will always buy into the lies of fear.

> Outsiders who come into community do not need to experience a group that seems perfect, but rather a community where grace abounds.

I began to experience true community for the first time during my first year of college. I formed relationships with Christian brothers who consistently practiced talking authentically about their sin and seeking help from one another. They freely spoke of their failures, which I thought were meant to be kept hidden.

Surprisingly, my first response to this type of confession was to continue to mask my sin. Why would I want to come clean with these guys? Would they like me if they really knew me? Over time it became clear that they valued being genuine with one another. Finally, after much resistance, I tried it. I came clean about my sin, which ushered in freedom and joy and put me on the path to discover the other virtues of community living.

THE BENEFITS OF TRUTH

Trust, commitment, prayer, and service are all vital aspects of community. But one value trumps them all: truth. Without truth there can be no trust, commitment, prayer, or service.

Honesty is fundamental for the well-being of biblical community, or any relationship for that matter (marriage, parenting, work, friendships). The depth believers experience with one another is linked directly to their level of honesty. Any relationship built on the façade of lies will surely crumble over time.

Outsiders who come into community do not need to experience a group that seems perfect, but rather a community where grace abounds. I'm part of a neighborhood group that gathers weekly. One of my neighbors, who isn't a Christian, but who has started to plug into the group with his family, recently told me, "Wow, you guys are all really messed up too." That sounds funny on the surface, but he was blown away by everyone's sincerity and authenticity. We all carry baggage, and community is the right place to unload it and help others unload as well.

Saying that is one thing; counting the benefits of truth in community is another. Here are four of them.

1. Truth allows people to know you. This is a basic, but vital, reality. Without truth people do not really know you but instead they know the caricature that you create. Social media exploits this reality. Through technological friendships mediated via our favorite social-media platform, you can present a visually enhanced version of yourself. They see your smiling kids, favorite vacations, perfectly cooked meals, and thoughtful insights. But do they know you? Of course not. They know the version you want them to see.

Only by entering your world, spending time with you, and hearing your hopes and dreams can they really know you. Imagine a couple who begins dating through an online service. They exchange emails, become Facebook friends, and talk to each other incessantly on the phone. Then the big night comes when they meet for the first time.

What if, after seeing the woman and having a face-to-face conversation, the guy were to say, "You seem nice, but I'd prefer to keep this thing online. I liked you much more from a distance"? End of relationship, right? Why is this? It's because authentic relationships require people to know each other deeply and not just from a distance.

2. Truth allows people to love you. Ironically, people who wear masks do not get the very thing they long for. They want love. But they can't receive it because whenever someone attempts to show them love, they believe the person is merely loving the mask, and not really loving them.

Sure, they like the clean version of me, the person might think. *But if they really knew me, they wouldn't love me.* One writer says it this way: "We will never feel love until we drop the act, until we're willing to show our true selves to the people around us."[2]

Honesty ushers in authentic love. Remember Paul's counsel to the church: "Let your love be genuine." Genuineness is reciprocal—as you are genuine with others, you can genuinely receive love from others. John Piper reminds us, "Love doesn't put up artificial fronts. Love does not dwell on the flaws of others. Love does not crave the praise of men. And love does not act religious to hide sin."[3]

Betsy had struggled with an eating disorder since her teenage years. People always told her she was beautiful, but she'd think, *No, I'm not. You just think I'm pretty because I'm skinny. If you only knew.* This all changed when she came clean to a woman in her small group about her struggle. Now when people tell her that she looks beautiful, she can hold her head high and think, *They know me and they still love me!*

3. Truth allows people to pray for you. Prayer is the most genuine expression of love. No amount of biblical community, in and of itself, can change the human heart. Only God can do that. But people can be a conduit of God's grace, most importantly by interceding on others' behalf. Honesty opens this conduit.

Prayer, for one, is impossible without honesty. If I do not know your real issues, how can I pray for you? Sure, I can mouth some vague generality like, "God, I pray that You would be with my buddy Zach." But what does that even mean? God is always with His children. We want to offer robust prayers informed by the genuineness of our brothers and sisters in Christ.

"God, I pray that You would protect Zach from the temptation of lust that he experiences while away on business travel" is a prayer rooted in honesty. We can pray specific prayers like, "God, I pray that You would encourage Jill as she struggles with discouragement as a stay-at-home mom." These prayers unleash God's aid. And they are impossible without honesty.

4. Truth allows people to help you. Paul reminds us that we fulfill the law of Christ as we bear one another's burdens (see Gal. 6:2). These types of burden-bearing relationships are possible only when we know what burdens we are to bear. We can see when someone is struggling against cancer or grieving the loss of a loved one. These are burdens the church should bear. But how about people groaning under the burden of worry, lust, unbelief, fear, or pride? These struggles may be easier to hide but they are no less weighty.

As people know you, they can find practical ways to offer support. To use our two examples above: help could come through calling your friend on a night when you know he is away on business travel and staying alone in a hotel. You may help Jill by inviting her to your house for some adult conversation while the kids play or by offering to babysit so that she and her husband could have a date night.

WARNING LIGHTS

On a personal level, as you work toward authenticity, you will find that you never outgrow your bent toward wearing masks. Even after you experience the joy of deep community, you will often find that you long to hide, cover your sin, and pretend that everything is fine.

On a relational level, honesty in community will often lead to a massive expenditure of time, energy, and effort. Not only that, but people will let you down. You will spend weeks loving someone as they attempt to be honest with you only to see them run and hide behind their mask again. You will find that you want to manipulate these relationships to bring about your desired outcome. You will long for people to be healthy and whole—and they will choose sin and rebellion. As Joseph H. Hellerman states:

> People who remain connected with their brothers and sisters in the local church almost invariably grow in self-understanding and they mature in their ability to relate in healthy ways to God and to their fellow human beings. This is especially the case for those courageous Christians who stick it out through the often messy process of interpersonal discord and conflict resolution. Long-term interpersonal relationships are the crucible of genuine progress in the Christian life. People who stay also grow. People who leave do not grow. It is a simple but profound biblical reality that we both grow and thrive together or we do not grow much at all.[4]

When you become weary over the messiness of community, remember that this is merely a small picture of what Jesus has done for His people. He has been long-suffering with His children, bearing our ongoing rebellion and persevering in His love. Consider how John motivated the early church to show love for one another:

> Beloved, let us love one another, for love is from God, and whoever loves has been born of God and knows God. Anyone who does not love does not know God, because God is love. In this the love of God was made manifest among us, that God sent his only Son into the world, so that we might live through him. In this is love, not that we have loved God but that he loved us and sent his Son to be the propitiation for our sins. Beloved, if God so loved us, we also ought to love one another. No one has ever seen God; if we love one another, God abides in us and his love is perfected in us. (1 John 4:7–12)

God demonstrates love to us so we demonstrate love to others. The messiness of honesty allows us to paint a picture of the way God loves His church.

Only by persevering over the long haul will we see genuine love produce personal transformation.

Emily, a typical college student, was unable to commit to anything. By her junior year she had changed majors four times, broken up with three boyfriends, and rotated between churches like a merry-go-round. She was attractive and likeable, but after a few minutes of conversation, you could tell that she was hiding something. Her most recent church stop led her to our church, and she was immediately pursued by a number of women about joining a small group. She would go but whenever the conversation shifted to her, she would give superficial, trite, and unclear answers. When people would press her for more, she would bail and move to another small group.

People in the church grew weary of her evasiveness. But Elizabeth stuck with her. She called her, texted her, took her to lunch, and never gave up. Finally one day Emily removed her mask and confessed the sin that others had committed against her as a child. She wept over the guilt and shame that clouded her understanding of God and the church.

Elizabeth's perseverance was rewarded with the fruit of Emily's life transformation. Often we undermine this process when we fail to do the hard, long work of fighting for honesty in relationships.

MOVING IN THE WAY OF TRUTH

So bring busted, messed up, sinful you into the light—knowing that God loves you in spite of your sin. Not only will God work in you, He will work *through* you to better serve others.

There is no magic pill for truth in community, nor are we likely to see everyone relinquish their masks overnight. But here are a few steps we can take to move toward honesty:

- Talk openly about your sin with those you trust. Rather than expecting other people to be vulnerable, you work to set the temperature for authenticity in your community. *People are more open when they have seen someone else model honesty.*

- Find ways to talk to people outside of the normal church gatherings. Invite someone to coffee, to lunch, or simply to hang out doing something you both enjoy. *People are more open when they are having fun.*
- Look out for when others are suffering. Loss, pain, or fear often prompts people to be more open about the reality of their heart. *People are more open when they hurt.*
- Serve alongside someone in mission. Consider projects such as painting a school, taking a meal to a widow, or tutoring in an after-school program. *People are more open when they have worked together.*
- Build deep relationships with the same people over a long period of time. Rather than shallow relationships with a wide array of folks, consistently pursue three or four people through ongoing interaction. *People are more open with those they trust.*

Through honest relationships we can experience the transformation that God offers. We can be free to love and be loved without hypocrisy. Why would we choose not to walk in that?

MISSION THREAD

The act of wearing a mask is exhausting. Imagine a community where people are loved for who they are and who Jesus is creating them to be. How beautiful would that be? Being in an unpretentious environment allows a person to see they are not alone in their battles. Others struggle and have been in similar places. That gives a lot of hope to people who know nothing but masks.

GETTING PRACTICAL

- **WHAT** mask are you still tempted to wear? What impression of yourself do you try to pass off to others?

- **WHAT'S** the first thing about yourself you typically try to work into a conversation with someone new? What does that mean for how you want to be portrayed?

- **WHAT** would it look like for you to take off your mask and be aggressively honest with your community? What conversations do you need to have?

"... Hate what is evil."

—ROMANS 12:9, NIV

CHAPTER 6

HATE CAN BE A GOOD THING

Many people consider hatred as a bad thing and in most circumstances it is. But not always. Sometimes, hate is an exceptionally good thing. For instance, Paul tells us to "hate what is evil" (Rom. 12:9 NIV).

Paul uses the word *evil* to denote anguish and fatality. He tells us to hate evil—to have an intense inward rejection of it. A gospel community hates what hurts anyone in their family. This causes them to do *whatever it takes* to confront that evil—especially when it's a family member's sin. Sincere love is foundational to successfully opposing others' sin.

We live in a world that believes in tolerance at all costs: we cannot love someone and oppose anything they are for or about. But we know that isn't how true love works. John Piper explains,

> You cannot be a wishy washy, lovey-dovey, relational non-hating anything person and be a loving person. A lot of people have that notion, that love is always smooth. Love is always easy. Love is always gentle. Love doesn't speak in negatives. Love doesn't get

on anyone's case. Love is just so soft and warm. *No way.* Not in this world. If you don't hate anything in this world, you cannot possibly love, because things are killing people. If you can't hate, you can't love.[1]

I'm not suggesting we create sin police who constantly bust people in their depravity. I am, however, encouraging us to become a people who love one another enough to hate the things that hurt us. God Himself demonstrates this type of overwhelming love that causes Him to hate evil.

A GOD WHO HATES

Many want to believe that a good God never hates anything and remains in a constant state of tolerance. They prefer a God who is warm, fuzzy, and has a little lamb that you can pet. Though I loved Mister Rogers (he was actually a godly man), Jesus is not wearing a cardigan and telling us that *it's a beautiful day in this neighborhood.*

The truth is that our God is good and He has an extremely resilient hatred. God hates. Let that sink in for a moment.

Our God is an intense warrior on a mission to destroy Satan, sin, and death. John tells us, "The reason the Son of God appeared was to destroy the works of the devil" (1 John 3:8). God removed Satan's sword (death), and He triumphed over it through the cross and an empty tomb. God did this because He loves us and hates the sin that enslaves and kills us (see John 8:34–35; Rom. 8:13). We see God's hatred for evil and simultaneously His pursuit of grace when the psalmist proclaims, "O you who love the LORD, hate evil! He preserves the lives of his saints; he delivers them from the hand of the wicked" (Ps. 97:10).

The good news of God's hatred is that He poured it out on His Son, not on those of us in Christ. Romans 3:23–25 says, "All have sinned and fall short of the glory of God, and all are justified freely by his grace through the redemption that came by Christ Jesus. God presented Christ as a sacrifice of atonement, through the shedding of his blood—to be received by faith" (NIV). We cannot grow numb or apathetic to this facet of the gospel.

God cannot love and turn a blind eye to the sin that wreaks havoc on His children and His world. He demonstrates hatred toward evil precisely because He loves. We, as the church, must hate as God hates.

EATING GLASS HURTS

Recently Renie and I were in our front yard, watching our kids play. All of a sudden two-year-old Piper picked up something shiny and small, about the size of a pea, and put it into her mouth. I had no idea what the object was, but I couldn't think of too many sparkling things lying on a driveway that would be good to eat. Then I realized the shiny object was glass.

In that moment Renie and I had a choice: do we stop Piper from ingesting the glass, or do we let her experience it for herself and maybe learn a life lesson?

Imagine if my wife and I had stopped to discuss the situation:

ME: "You tell her. I don't want to hurt her feelings."

RENIE: "No, you stop her. She may get mad at me, and I don't want that."

ME: "But if I say something, she may cry and then I have to deal with the emotional scars."

RENIE: "That's true, plus this really is a problem she's gotten herself into."

ME: "Maybe the glass won't hurt her that much."

RENIE: "She'll probably be okay, plus I don't want to run over there. It's just too much effort right now."

ME: "It's been a long day and let's be honest, she has to learn these things on her own."

Would this type of reaction make us good parents or bad parents?

Absolutely horrible parents! Yet this is the stance many Christians take. Herein lies one of the primary reasons Christian growth is often stunted and genuine community is hindered. We do not take the same aggressive stance toward sin that Renie and I must take with that piece of glass. The glass is shiny and looks appealing, but as appealing as it may be, it's glass and it is not meant for chewing or digesting. Not only could it cut her lips, tongue, and gums; if she were to swallow the glass, it could do countless damage to her insides.

Sin, like that piece of glass, quickly moves from something appealing to something destructive. We may walk through life with Christians who are on the brink of eating glass, and yet we idly watch addictions start, affairs occur, self-injury continue, disrespect run wild. We stand back as destruction tears people down. We rationalize:

> *I don't want to hurt her feelings.*
> *It's not my place.*
> *He needs to learn this for himself.*
> *I have enough problems.*
> *It's not my business.*
> *I don't want to lose our friendship.*
> *She'll figure it out eventually.*

Meanwhile, the person we are called to love just ate glass. But we are more concerned about ourselves than we are about the well-being of the person we are called to serve.

Will you potentially hurt their feelings? Will they get mad? Will they hold it against you? Will you get hurt in the process? Will you lose their friendship?

Yes, that is possible. Those things may happen. Hating what is evil includes challenging them about that which is killing them. So the casualty of losing a friendship is worth the loss if it means stopping someone from dying in sin.

To be clear, I am not issuing us a spiritual jerk card. I'm asking that we check our motives for why and how we love people by hating the things that hurt them. This type of hatred is vital for biblical community to thrive. The less we care about hating sin, the less we experience authentic and world-changing community.

CONFRONTING SIN

As my daughter placed the shiny object into her mouth, my wife and I ran as fast as we could to her, yelling, "STOP!"

Renie grabbed Piper, and I raked her mouth as quickly as I could. I could see the confusion and fear in my little girl's eyes. Thankfully, I was able to retrieve the glass just before she swallowed it. Even though we grabbed it before it could do any real damage, she still suffered some cuts and she didn't understand why her parents just put her in a headlock. I was grateful that all we experienced were a few tears, some confusion, and a cut or two rather than something far worse. My hope is that we will build similar communities where we reduce the number of fatalities while collectively dealing with the cuts.

The Bible is clear when it comes to confronting other believers who are in sin. Jesus told us, "Pay attention to yourselves! If your brother sins, rebuke him" (Luke 17:3). Rebuking means to charge sharply. Jesus was not pulling punches here, or when He said, "If your brother sins against you, go and tell him his fault, between you and him alone. If he listens to you, you have gained your brother" (Matt. 18:15). While these passages are straightforward, sometimes it is challenging to apply them. Here are some steps to take when confronting someone's sin.

1. Examine your own life.

Don't judge me. This statement has become our culture's mantra. Even Jesus warned us to be careful how we judge others: "Judge not, that you be not judged. For with the judgment you pronounce you will be judged, and with the measure you use it will be measured to you" (Matt. 7:1–2). Context is key. The word *judge* within this framework means to pronounce another person guilty before God. It is calling another guilty from a place of pride and condemnation.

Jesus said, "Why do you see the speck that is in your brother's eye, but do not notice the log that is in your own eye? Or how can you say to your brother, 'Let me take the speck out of your eye,' when there is the log in your own eye? You hypocrite" (Matt. 7:3–5).

Jesus emphatically rejected our prideful judgment. He cautioned us to look at our own prevalent sin before we confront someone else's. We must inspect the malice of our own ways. Confessing our sin to God and then to others is the first step (see James 5:16). The second step is to dig to our root motivation for why we want to confront the other person: Is there selfish ambition? Do we confront to make ourselves feel less guilty about our own faults?

It becomes easier to ignore our sin when we consistently point out everyone else's. In Matthew 7:5, Jesus continued: "First take the log out of your own eye, and then you will see clearly to take the speck out of your brother's eye."

But Jesus did not stop there. He said that once you examine yourself, then you go to your brother or sister and address their sin. Your sin doesn't render you impotent to address someone else's sin. Humble confession of your sin positions you to have maximum impact.

You may not feel spiritual, but the reality is that your repentant heart frees you to help your weaker brother or sister entangled in sin. Your humble confession about how you neglected loving and serving your wife, for instance, positions you to address the passive, demanding husband in your small group who is crushing his wife under the weight of his expectations. Your repentance surrounding an eating disorder positions you to offer hope to a teenaged girl in the same position. God, in His sovereignty, has arranged your community such that your places of brokenness can be a unique source of strength to others. As Galatians 6:1 reminds, "If anyone is caught in any transgression, you who are spiritual should restore him in a spirit of gentleness."

The church is called to challenge sin. But we must acknowledge our own sin first and then confront others' sins with a spirit of love and a desire for restoration.

2. Confront in love (don't be a jerk).

Not long into my pastorate, I had to journey with a young man and woman who, though believers, were actively living in sin. The church leaders followed the process, outlined in Matthew 18, for dealing with sin. First we confronted them privately. Next, we took a close friend along with us to challenge them. Then because we saw no signs of repentance, we humbly brought the matter before our church family and asked them to pray that the couple would repent and seek restoration. During that process, the church leaders and I received a life's worth of pushback from other believers, telling us that we needed to stop judging them.

Ephesians 4:25 tells us to declare truth to those within our community: "Having put away falsehood, let each one of you speak the truth with his neighbor, for we are members one of another." We must speak that truth in love, otherwise our words will sound abrasive.

I relish playing the drums. Any time I see a drum set, within minutes I'm sitting on the drum throne doing my thing. By "doing my thing," I do not mean playing skillfully. I have no clue how to play the drums. I just like the idea of banging on the toms and the cymbals. The rooms I play in tend to empty out fairly quickly. While I'm in my "zone," there is nothing enjoyable for others. It's just noise. Paul compares this style of playing to what happens when we confront others without loving them: "If I speak in the tongues of men and of angels, but have not love, I am a noisy gong or a clanging cymbal" (1 Cor. 13:1).

Do you struggle with people running when you confront and speak truth into their lives? At times they may not want to hear your concerns no matter how kindly you communicate, but more often they may struggle with the way you present the message. I have this challenge. My wife and many others tell me that I seek controversy. I constantly have to check my argumentative nature and make sure my motive is for the other person's wellbeing, not for my desire to get in a fight. I need to heed the proverb, which counsels, "As charcoal to hot embers and wood to fire, so is a quarrelsome man for kindling strife" (Prov. 26:21).

Speaking in love does not mean watering down the truth—it means communicating from a place of humility. The goal is not to start a fire or to clang cymbals, but to love the person well with the same kindness that Christ has offered you, so that they have the opportunity to accurately hear the help you seek to give them.

3. Don't quit.

Have you ever dealt with someone who drained the life out of you? Did you want to quit on the person? I have. I'm not proud of it, but I do know that if you haven't been tempted to quit, then you have probably never walked in true community. I have said many times that leading biblical community would be a breeze if people were not involved. We love to throw around the "Christian" coffee cup verses like Proverbs 27:17—"Iron sharpens iron, and one man sharpens another" —but we have to pause long enough to consider the implications of walking in deep community, where we are willing to be stick it out with one another.

If God has designed us for one another's refining then we must be intentional and consistent in our contact. If one piece of iron hangs in a corner while the other sits on a workbench in the middle of the room, both pieces remain dull.

> Building genuine community and actively seeking mission will never be easy.

Sharpening iron can be intense; it isn't easy as sparks fly. Not only that, but actively hating the things that hurt those with whom we are in community is not only inconvenient, it can be exhausting. We must remember Paul's exhortation to "not grow weary of doing good, for in due season we will reap, if we do not give up" (Gal. 6:9).

Recently after speaking to a room full of retirees, an eighty-nine-year-old man came up to me and said, "Son, I have two words for you as you walk with others: *Don't quit!*"

Building genuine community and actively seeking mission will never be easy because people will quit on you, turn their backs on you, and abandon the mission you thought you were both sharing. They will climb up in the tree and say they want to jump from the limb. You will plead and tell them why it's a terrible idea, and after much pleading, they will jump, hit the ground, and break their leg—then look at you and ask if you can take them to the hospital. Twelve weeks later, you will look outside to see that same person standing on the limb with a perfectly healed leg and with the thought of jumping again. Don't quit.

Samuel had dealt with an addiction to over-the-counter pills since he was fourteen years old. Through a series of events I ended up watching college football with this guy. Not long after that, I met him for breakfast and we discussed the reasons he had initially turned to pills. We continued to get together, and most of the time, I noticed that Samuel had bloodshot eyes, because he had taken a cocktail of pills beforehand. Numerous times I played the tough-love card and got up and left. I threatened not to meet with him anymore, and then he would come back clean the next time.

When he reached a month of being clean, we celebrated his victory. The next day, he called to inform me that he was high again. Samuel needed professional drug rehab, so I drove him to the treatment facility, checked him in, met with doctors, and paid the fee. I thought, *This is it. This time it's going to happen.*

Seven hours later, in the middle of the night, Samuel called to tell me he had broken out of the facility and was now hitchhiking to another state. Two things went through my head in that moment: *I like my sleep, and I don't like Samuel anymore.* I wanted to quit on him. It is only by the Holy Spirit's power that I picked up that punk that night. I showed some tough love, but by God's grace, I didn't quit. I would love to tell you that Samuel is well and leading mission teams to Malaysia, but he is still actively battling his addictions.

Paul tells us, "If anyone is caught in any transgression, you who are spiritual should restore him in a spirit of gentleness" (Gal. 6:1). But in the next verse he challenges us: "Bear one another's burdens, and so fulfill the law of Christ." We are called to endure others' afflictions—to carry something troublesome that isn't even ours, to make it our own.

The only power that can propel this type of burden-bearing love is through the Holy Spirit's reminders of the One who bore the weight of sin, fully and finally, on His back on the cross. Jesus bore the weight of our sin and this gives us the strength to bear with others. Don't quit.

4. Restore and pray.

By God's grace, as we hate what is evil and confront sin that destroys, we will experience the joy of helping people climb down from the tree and not jump. In other words, we will see confession and repentance become a reality. This is the hope of any confrontation, and it does happen!

Many years ago my friend Lee confronted me when I was complaining to him about work and marriages stresses. I had been married only a few months and was dealing with a boss who was getting under my skin. I had a bitter attitude. Lee knew me well and discerned that something else was at the root of my defiance and cynicism.

Out of nowhere it seemed, Lee said, "What sin are you in?"

I popped right back with something smart-alecky. But he kept pressing.

Finally, he said, "Are you looking at porn?"

Lee knew that I was manipulating his impressions with crafty words and masking my failure with pride. Lee loved me enough not to quit on me and not to let me continue in my sin. He told me that I needed to tell my wife what I had done.

Of course I pushed back, which made him confront me more. He ended our conversation by telling me that he loved me as a brother and then he prayed that I would have the courage to be honest and vulnerable with Renie. He didn't simply confront, he wanted to restore me. The goal of humbly confronting sin in others is *always* restoration.

After much contemplation, I confessed to Renie that I had sinned against God and against her by looking at pornography. She cried, she questioned, she punched me in my gut as hard as I've ever been punched, and then she prayed over me.

Though I had confessed my sin to God and felt His forgiveness, in that moment I felt healed (see 1 John 1:9). I experienced the reality of

James 5:16: "Confess your sins to one another and pray for one another, that you may be healed." By God's grace, confession brings healing and prompts a desire in us to pray for one another. James reminds us that "the prayer of a righteous person has great power." So as we are aware of sin in others, the best way to bear their burdens is to work toward restoration and to pray.

We cannot be a generation who says, "I'll pray for you," and then never prays. During our membership meetings (we called them "family meetings") at the church I pastored, we set aside time for confrontation and confession. That may sound crazy—and the first time we tried, it was as awkward as it could get. We didn't have low lighting or soft guitar picking. Just fluorescent lights, old metal chairs, and silence. It felt like an eternity of deafening stillness. And then I heard the most amazing sound.

One single metal chair slid across the tile floor, and not long after that, the room filled with the sound of people confessing and being prayed for. Those prayers trumped the sound of the metal chair and became the most beautiful sound I have ever heard. The level of care taking place in that room is what the world yearns for.

> The Holy Spirit is powerful and active, and we must trust His work and never confuse ourselves for Him.

We eventually quit setting aside time for this because it became the everyday culture of our amazing community. Confession and prayer leads to restoration. We do not hold people's sins over their head or banish them forever from the table of the Lord. We restore them, as Christ did with us, to a position of honor. Restore one another with affirming words and caring actions, and then watch God do what only He can with the prayers of His people: heal.

5. Trust God to Work.

We must always remember our role in this process. Many have a savior complex and feel as though their role is to save people from their misery. I have found myself in this place many times and know an important part of confronting and restoring is to set clear boundaries. You and I are called to do a certain job only. We cannot heal or stop them from sinning. Only God in His kindness can move a person from sin into newness (see Rom. 2:4; 2 Cor. 5:17). We can act as roadblocks, warning lights, caution tape, and voices of reason, but we are not God's Spirit.

The Holy Spirit is powerful and active, and we must trust His work and never confuse ourselves for Him. God is always moving in ways that you and I may never know. The Bible pictures the work of God like a wind, blowing to and fro, wherever it pleases. This is the way God acts in our feeble efforts at confronting sin as well. Behind our efforts He is pursuing, convicting, challenging, and shaping all things to fulfill His good purposes. Let's not get in His way, but work to fulfill our jobs and let Him do His.

MISSION THREAD

Society says to let people live however they want, but too often people look back at situations that led to despair and wonder, *Why didn't anyone warn me or help me?* Imagine a community where people care enough for one another to say the hard things, and as a result prevent a lot of pain and heartache. Everyone wants someone in their corner, and though it is countercultural, at its core, this type of community is attractive to a hurting world, because it reflects a God who loves us so deeply that He hates the thing that hurts us most: sin.

GETTING PRACTICAL

- **WHAT** sin do you need to hate (and confess and repent of) in your life before you approach others about their sin?
- **WHEN** considering confrontation, have you found yourself thinking any of the below statements? If so, in what situations?

I don't want to hurt their feelings.
It's not my place.
He needs to learn this for himself.
I have enough problems.
It's not my business.
I don't want to lose our friendship.
She'll figure it out eventually.

- **IN** light of hating the sin that hurts those you love, what conversations do you need to have?

". . . hold fast to what is good."

—ROMANS 12:9

CHAPTER 7

GLUE TO THE GOOD

I t is not enough simply to confront sin. We must also intentionally build communities that actively encourage and affirm one another in the areas where God is at work. These two acts—challenging sin and encouraging godliness—join together to create healthy gospel communities.

Imagine that you are friends with Sarah. Sarah is a new Christian and is battling demons from her past, which was filled with poor decisions and painful consequences. Her life is messy. Each day she struggles with the temptation to return to her former life—and some days she loses. What does Sarah need most from you? Does she need steady reminders of her foolish choices and constant prodding to try harder and be better?

No. What she needs most is ongoing, daily reminders and evidence of God's grace in her life. Even if the steps are small or short-lived, one of the best ways to fight sin is to cheer on godliness. We all know that we are more likely to pursue a certain way of life if we find joy and reassurance in it. While shame and guilt over sin may produce change for a moment, encouragement can bring lasting transformation.

Throughout Scripture we see Christians encouraging one another in godliness. In *Practicing Affirmation*, Sam Crabtree highlights the way Jesus and Paul practiced encouragement:

Jesus Affirms

- He calls His disciples "salt" and "light" (Matt. 5:13–14)
- He says His listeners are more valuable than sparrows (Matt. 10:31)
- He commends a woman for her great faith (Matt. 15:28)
- He applauds the woman of ill repute for doing a beautiful thing (Mark 14:6)
- He marvels at a soldier's faith (Luke 7:9)
- He praises John the Baptist, saying he is the greatest man who ever lived (Luke 7:28)
- He endorses a widow's generosity (Luke 21:3–4)
- He commends Nathanael for not being a hypocrite (John 1:47)

Paul Affirms

- He praises Phoebe for her servant ways (Rom. 16:1–2)
- He applauds the Corinthians for their faithful remembrance of traditions (1 Cor. 11:2)
- He refers to Titus as his beloved child (Titus 1:4)
- He thanks God for the Philippian church (Phil. 1:3)
- He encourages Timothy to persevere and not let anyone look down on him for his age (1 Tim. 4:12)[1]

And in Romans 12:9, Paul encourages us to "hold fast to what is good" or to "cling to what is good," depending on the translation. The English phrase *hold fast* or *cling to* comes from the Greek word *kollaō*, which means to glue.

As we have seen, Paul's commands are not directed toward individual practice, but are meant to be accomplished in biblical community. Paul's statement here is no exception: we must actively glue ourselves to the good we see in others.

This means that the church should be the most encouraging group of people we could be around. Life is hard, right? We have plenty going on to discourage us since we constantly make mistakes and others hurt us. This combination of factors is enough to make anyone feel defeated. But the church is God's gift to keep you encouraged! When you are around God's people, you should find joy, hear affirming words, and be reminded of your blessings.

"Bro, I can't believe how good you are at that. God has given you a wonderful gift."

"I see definite growth in you in that area."

"Friends, we have so much to be thankful for!"

Words such as these should echo through our communities.

But can a person be good? If we aren't careful, we could misconstrue what Paul means by *good*. This is not the idea of clinging to your inner good. The last thing I want to do is build a Dr. Phil or Oprah philosophy for the church. As I've repeated throughout this book, we must interpret Scripture with Scripture. The word *good* in Romans 12 is the same as the good we find in Mark 10:18: "Why do you call me good? No one is good except God alone."

Paul also clarified this idea in Romans 3:10 (quoting Ps. 14:1–3): "None is righteous, no, not one." Our calling finds its origin in God, because in God alone we discover the exclusive dwelling of good.

GOD GIVES US HIS GOOD

God has not withheld His blessings but has lavished them on us for His glory.

- God takes the selfish and makes them selfless.
- God takes the prideful and marks them with humility.
- God takes the apathetic and overwhelms them with passion.
- God takes the abuser and brings about kindness.
- God takes the violent and creates in them meekness.
- God takes the cheater and transforms them to honesty.
- God takes all of our wrong and gives us all of His right.

God gives us His good in the place of our selfishness, pride, apathy, and foolishness.

For each of the above scenarios you can probably place a specific person's name where you have seen God do that exact work in them. As God changes people, they flee sin and pursue holiness. They are no longer the same and that is worth celebrating.

While pastoring, I became friends with a college student, Ben. Ben was about one thing: himself. But over the years I watched God take away Ben's selfishness and replace it with a spirit of sacrifice. It was a full-scale heart renovation. He stopped looking out for number 1. Instead of hitting every campus party, he filled his time going to high-school lunches and investing in the students God placed in his path.

What helped with that change? People in our community spoke consistent and intentional support, which encouraged him in the mission God was accomplishing in him. God worked through the community's affirming words to help him realize the blessings of his transformation. We must build this kind of culture where we celebrate what we see God doing.

SIX LITTLE WORDS

Whenever you have witnessed this kind of transformation, have you verbally acknowledged it to that person? Are you creating a daily culture of encouragement and gluing to the good? Do you make it an intentional part of the rhythm of your life?

Hebrews 3:13 tells us to "encourage one another daily, as long as it is called 'Today'" (NIV). Each day, God's people should make it a discipline to find ways to encourage others.

We have an abundance of ways to do just that. With the push of a few buttons we can send someone a text message pointing out an evidence of God's grace in their lives. A brief phone call can be a tool to offer hope or joy. A handwritten note can go a long way to communicate that we took the time and effort to bless someone. ("Liking" something on Facebook or retweeting a tweet does not equal spiritual encouragement—I'm sure this is somewhere in the Bible.)

But don't rely on technology or notes alone. The best way to encourage another person is face-to-face. Think of the people you will see on a given day and find a way to point out evidences of God's grace within them.

> Biblical encouragement uses your words to point out examples of God's goodness in another person's life.

The word *encourage* in Hebrews 3 has nothing to do with the new haircut and outfit someone has or the cool truck they are driving. There is a significant difference between complimenting someone and encouraging them in Christ. I am all for compliments but no amount of compliments can replace one act of biblical encouragement. Biblical encouragement uses your words to point out examples of God's goodness in another person's life.

When I was a college sophomore, during spring break at Daytona Beach, my friend Kristie spoke clear and blunt truth into my life: "You do not have to wait to do something significant for God. You should go ahead and begin pursuing ministry right here, right now, because God has gifted you to do it, and there is no reason you can't. Don't wait. I see God working in you."

God used those last six words—*I see God working in you*—to change my life trajectory.

The power of those six little words may be the drop of water that starts the tidal wave of transformation in your wife, your son, your best friend, or that socially awkward guy in your small group. Have you experienced that "I see God working in you" moment from another's words? Those moments in time are irreplaceable, and we have the privilege to be the ones who generate those moments for others.

Proverbs 18:21 states, "Death and life are in the power of the tongue." We know that there is death in words. People use their words all the time to tear down and destroy. At some point, all of us have been the victim of harsh words.

Words can also bring life. There is life-giving authority in the words we use as we help spur on one another toward maturity in Christ and the mission He has given.

- When you observe a husband serving his wife, who normally struggles to give of himself, make it a clear point to tell him. Glue to the good.
- When you see a mother, who fights to have patience with her four-year-old, have an extra measure of tolerance, tell her that you notice the hard work she does. Glue to the good.
- When you see someone take responsibility where guidance has been lacking, speak affirming words into their leadership. Glue to the good.
- When you watch a student make the decision to seek Jesus rather than give way to peer pressure, tell them that God is glorified in the wisdom they are applying. Glue to the good.
- When you notice a person, who struggles with apathy, step up to live life on mission, write a note and confirm the work that God is living out through them. Glue to the good.

As we do this we will be privileged to see stronger marriages, more patient parents, committed relationships, devoted leaders, emboldened missionaries, and a richer community. As author Sam Crabtree states in *Practicing Affirmation*, "God is glorified in us when we affirm the work He has done and is doing in others."[2]

WHY DON'T WE GLUE TO THE GOOD?

It is difficult to be encouraging because, well . . . we are selfish. We recognize the value that comes from praising others, but we don't take the time to do it. Our selfishness comes out in a number of ways.

Comparison condition

I am as competitive as they come. It doesn't matter if I'm playing Go Fish or just driving to lunch with coworkers, I want to win. I love being able to yell, "Go fish!" and I love arriving to the lunch destination first. My tendency to be overly competitive reveals that I struggle with comparison. Unfortunately, I've also come to understand the truth of Mark Twain's statement: "Comparison is the death of joy."[3]

Comparison is the killer to authentic encouragement. It feels ridiculous even to have to confess this, but I even struggle with comparing myself with others who live on mission. My friend Micah recently told me about an opportunity he had to share the gospel with some neighbors, and my initial reaction was to think about the last time I was able to share the gospel.

What is wrong with me? I totally discounted the fact that the gospel was shared with a couple who need God's grace because my attention was on me! I suffer from comparison condition. It took me until the next day to speak words of support to Micah.

Micah needs those affirming words—not because he is insecure, but because God has designed us in such a way that we need one another. I failed him as a brother because I was caught up in equating his steps of faith to a lack of my own. Comparison is like acetone to glue—it eradicates the tackiness and effectiveness of it. It drives us from gluing to the good.

> Comparison is the killer to authentic encouragement.

Dude disorder

A second reason we let our selfishness prevent us from being encouraging is what I call "dude disorder." If you are a guy, you may think that pursuing the ideas in this chapter feels similar to signing other dudes' high school yearbooks. When one was shoved in front of me, I would think, *You're telling me I have to affirm something I've observed in this person's life? Can't I just tell him to have a good summer, stay cool, and see him on the football field?* Now, we'd sign a girl's yearbook in a heartbeat and say all kinds of encouraging things (most of which we didn't mean). But a guy's yearbook? Totally different story.

This is an area where guys need to man-up. I know this chapter deals with encouragement, and I am ultimately seeking that by calling out us fellas and combating the pride that runs rampant among us. Pride not only blocks our capacity to receive correction, it also hinders our ability to affirm. Men, we must lead in speaking sustaining truth to the other men we do life with. It's time to quit hiding behind our wives' faith and pioneer a culture of gluing to the good.

Too often Christian small groups consist of meeting over a meal where the men verbally zing one another, and then when the time comes to talk about the Bible and real life, they become mute. Rather than trying to outwit our brothers and show everyone else how snarky we can be, what if we spoke graciously and kindly to one another? Think about what brings hope and joy to you. Is it when one of your buddies busts your chops in front of your coworkers, ending in a room filled with laughter? Or is it when a buddy goes out of his way to tell you that you are doing a good job, he is proud of you, and counts it a joy to be your friend? The answer is clear. So why do we fail to do for others what we find most encouraging?

The culture of the church I pastored in Columbia, South Carolina, completely changed when for a season we transitioned all of our small groups to be gender specific. No longer could the men hide in the shadows of their wives' relationship with Jesus. The masks were off and life-giving conversations began to spring up among them. Authentic community—with its confession, restoration, and giftings—began to happen as men spoke supporting truth to one another and found themselves in the shadows of a grace-giving cross. I believe the spiritual development in our men became the catalyst that moved us into an incredible season of growth.

Our church grew, leaders developed, and other small groups formed, which replicated the level of community that these men developed.

In Genesis, man was placed in the garden to create and cultivate. Men, lead in creating and cultivating communities who glue to the good. The application is simple: look for God at work in others and aggressively point it out to them.

Nearsightedness

Finally, you can't glue to the good if you can't see it, and you can't see it if you aren't looking beyond yourself. Too many of us struggle from what I call spiritual nearsightedness. Nearsightedness is where you are not able to see distances away from yourself.

The Holy Spirit has given us eyes to see how He is working in others, and we must obediently focus to look for it. My favorite comedian Brian Regan does a piece called "Me Monster," where he describes people who always draw attention off others and back to themselves. It is hilarious, but carries a sobering truth. It is time to put the "Me Monster" to death.

Kevin and Beth's marriage was in trouble. They had been married almost a decade, and with each subsequent year things got worse. Kevin was a workaholic, who never seemed to notice Beth's needs. Beth, on the other hand, was overly assertive, crushing Kevin under the weight of selfish expectations and guilt.

One weekend they participated in a conference at a local church. In God's kindness, that weekend was filled with honest conversation about the challenges of marriage. Kevin and Beth heard stories of how God had transformed people who had struggled just as they did. During a prayer time, Kevin was asked to pray with a buddy who was going through a particularly daunting time in his marriage. God changed Kevin's heart that night. For the first time in a long time, he took his eyes off himself and prayed for someone else. His feeble attempts to support his brother in Christ caused him to see his own shortcomings and then to pursue a joy-filled time of confession and healing with Beth.

It's amazing what can happen if you take your eyes off yourself and all that is broken in life and attempt to be a source of encouragement to others. Not only does God use this to bring affirmation to someone else's life, but it brings joy to yours as well.

MISSION THREAD

Encouragement toward the good things of God is attractive to our increasingly cynical society. As gospel communities build up people in the right things, we send them into the world with a humble confidence. People want to be part of a group that not only cares enough to confront the bad but also loves enough to encourage them toward the good God is working in them. This is appealing to those who do not yet believe the gospel because they will see the good of God by the way we love one another through our words.

GETTING PRACTICAL

- **VAGUE** notions of "I really need to be more encouraging" rarely result in action. What works is noticing someone next to you at lunch, thinking about an evidence of God's grace in her life, and speaking it to her right then. What would it take to commit to daily encourage someone else?
- **HOW** do you feel when someone sends you a handwritten note? Do you think someone you write to would appreciate it as well?
- **WHAT** is stopping you from taking someone to coffee for the sole purpose of calling out the good you see God doing in them?

Life in Community

"Love one another with brotherly affection. Outdo one another in showing honor."

ROMANS 12:10

CHAPTER 8

LOVE, LIKE, AND HONOR

Though the cover of this book depicts an ideal, harmonious meal shared with drama-free friends, don't be fooled. I know people. You know people.

We are surrounded by them every day. We are one of them. There is no magic, *Leave It to Beaver* group of people who always get along.

These people may all smile for the picture, giving the appearance of relational bliss, but just beforehand some were probably arguing, crying, angry, or frustrated.

Imagine yourself at a reunion where everyone shows up—even that random distant cousin you've never met—and you find yourself surrounded by an eclectic group you're supposed to call family. Some are socially draining and make you want to scout out a seat at the opposite end of the table. Some are harsh, while others irritate you because you never know what they are thinking. A few saunter to the table, demonstrating their propensity for habitual tardiness. The type-A folks harbor angst toward the *late people* as the food is now cold, the ice has melted, and the tea is diluted. And of course there are those you try to avoid, as they are only looking for a good argument.

I don't know about you, but with a lot of relationships I find myself thinking, *I have to love them, but I don't have to like them.* If you're honest, you have probably felt the same sentiment.

That idea sounds nice, but it is far from biblical. Paul tells us that we are to "love one another with brotherly affection" (Rom. 12:10). This verse is not pointing us toward a *just put up with them* kind of love. It references a mutual tender affection for one another. Paul's directive is that we are to actually care about them.

I can serve others without having an affection or like for them, and then play that off as loving them but not having to like them. But God calls us to truly like one another. So in the midst of a table full of type-A, late, passive-aggressive, overly talkative, harsh, rude, opinionated, and awkward people, we must seek to love *and* like one another.

The only problem is that this seems impossible.

Think about it. Can you make yourself have a specific emotion toward a person? I'm not talking about a fake smile or an empty compliment. Can you conjure up feelings toward others?

The Scriptures tell us you can.

IN VIEW OF GOD'S MERCY

Imagine that you are seven years old. You've been riding with your family all day headed toward the beach, and you've had to endure your little brother for the entire drive. Not a car ride has gone by that he hasn't thrown something at you, punched you, or made it known over and over that he is not touching you. "I'm not touching! I'm not touching! *I'm not touching!*" as his sticky little hand waves within an inch of your face. Your brother seemingly has one job in life: to annoy you—and he's good at it. He hasn't done much in his five years to make you like him.

Finally, your dad pulls into the parking lot across from the beach. It's hot, the humidity is thick, and the beach breeze feels more like the air from a blistering heater.

You carry the heavy cooler to your traditional spot just beyond the pier, while your brother carries nothing and tries to trip you the entire walk. When you arrive, you and your dad immediately drop into the sand and begin your yearly tradition of building a sand castle. Meanwhile your brother throws sand in your direction, trying to get some in your eyes.

Somehow amid the distraction, after an hour's worth of work, you and your dad complete your best sand castle yet. People comment on the detail in which you crafted the bridge, the moat, and the shell-covered towers. You beam as you are showered with compliments. The sweat turns to salt on your face, but the effort seems worth it as you look at what you've just created.

And then your little brother jumps from the top of the cooler (that you carried) right into the middle of your masterpiece. The sand that once stood as a prized masterpiece now settles as a pile of . . . well, just a pile of sand.

Of course, this angers you, but it's typical of what your brother always does. He has only given you another reason not to like him. The sweat on your face is now mixed with tears. Your dad encourages you to cool off, so you make your way to the water and wade in waist deep.

But ten miles offshore, a storm is brewing, creating a dangerous undertow in the shallow water along the shore. The current begins to pull you into the deep, and you don't have the strength to do anything about it. You are now in over your head. The push and pull of the current throws your body into a state of panic, and you quickly lose the ability to tell which way is up. Yelling only draws water into your mouth, threatening to drown you. It is a fight, and you are not winning. Your muscles cramp, you are tumbling along the ocean floor with death looming.

Without warning, two strong hands scoop you out of the dangerous currents. You wrap your arms around your dad's shoulders as he carries you to the safety of the beach. You choke up water and struggle to breathe, but slowly oxygen fills your lungs.

As your dad puts you down, you see your little brother running frantically toward you, yelling, "You're okay!"

Right then your little brother is precious to you. Tears stream down

> As we become people who see life as a gift and not something we are entitled to, we will view people through a completely different lens.

your face as you and your brother celebrate that you are truly okay. Moments earlier you wanted to poke out his eye and now you find yourself embracing him.[1]

That's the kind of perspective God wants us to have toward our brothers and sisters in Christ. And we can achieve that only when we realize that spiritually we were once drowning, but God reached down and saved us—to which our spiritual family members rejoiced. That understanding—viewing life through the lens of God's mercy—directs our souls toward an affection that at first seems unreasonable.

We worship with one another *in view of God's mercy.*
We sacrifice for one another *in view of God's mercy.*
We walk in humility with one another *in view of God's mercy.*
We authentically love one another *in view of God's mercy.*
We hate the evil that hurts others *in view of God's mercy.*
We cling to the good we see in one another *in view of God's mercy.*
We show affection to one another *in view of God's mercy.*

Within community we sit at a table with others, understanding that death was imminent but because of God's compassion, we have life.

As we become people who see life as a gift and not something we are entitled to, we will view people through a completely different lens. And as we grow deeper into the depths of God's mercies, we will discover that our life is also given to us to be given away to others. In other words, the gift of life should not make us "me-centric" but rather "others-centric." God's mercy affords us the ability even to show affection to those we may not like.

So in response to the earlier question about whether you can force yourself to feel specific emotions toward another: the answer is no, you can't force yourself. But you can pray for a correct perspective of yourself and of them, which will help you see them in a fuller, more accurate light.

As C. S. Lewis says, you can practically do the things you would do for them if you did feel that affection toward them, and in all likelihood that affection will begin to grow as you love and serve them. Lewis's illustration to this point is particularly helpful. He describes our feelings and actions as a train. If our feelings are the caboose that drive our actions (the cars on the train), then we will be in trouble. If our actions are the caboose (i.e., we do the right things), then our feelings will follow.

> The rule for all of us is perfectly simple. Do not waste time bothering whether you "love" your neighbor; act as if you did. As soon as we do this we find one of the great secrets. When you are behaving as if you loved someone, you will presently come to love him. If you injure someone you dislike, you will find yourself disliking him more. If you do him a good turn, you will find yourself disliking him less.[2]

Is this difficult? Yes.

Is it possible? Yes.

Take a minute now and ask the Holy Spirit to help you want this perspective.

FORBEAR AND FORGIVE

We see this process often in marriage counseling. One spouse offends the other deeply, perhaps through an emotional attachment or an affair. There, sitting in my office, are two wounded, discouraged, and fed-up people.

By God's grace, even a couple with pain this deep can demonstrate the type of love that God has for His people. Like the prophet Hosea, a spouse can forgive and choose to love his wayward wife. I don't suggest that this road will be easy. It will be paved by brokenness, doubt, mistrust, and anger. It will take time and much grace for the relationship to heal.

On a smaller scale, this type of pain is sure to come to everyone living in biblical community. People will let you down, hurt you, sin against you, and be hard to love. They will continually annoy you. I can guarantee that little brother from the beach will be back to his old ways by the next day. This causes us to practice forgiveness and to remember how often God forgives us.

People will throw sand your direction—and yet it's possible that you both love and like them. Fortunately, for you and me, as others grow in their understanding of mercy, they might even like us (who can be unlikable) too. As we reset our minds to see one another through a lens of mercy, forgiveness will become a part of the community we are building. The Scriptures are rich with the thread of the mercy that leads us to a place of deep forgiveness. Consider that

> [We] are justified by his grace as a gift, through the redemption that is in Christ Jesus, whom God put forward as a propitiation by [Christ's] blood, to be received by faith. This was to show God's righteousness, because in his divine forbearance he had passed over former sins. (Rom. 3:24–25)

With Jesus as our example, we can have forbearance (patience) and forgiveness for those who hurt us. Often we think, *But they haven't done anything to warrant my forgiveness or they haven't sat by themselves long enough and thought about what they have done.*

For genuine love to work, it must not keep a record of wrongs (see 1 Cor. 13:5 NIV). The couple mentioned earlier would surely see their hopes of restoration crumble if one were to say to the other: "You'll have to earn my love again. If you do enough good things to show me that you love me, then I'll give this relationship another try."

Forgiveness means that we give up the right to hold a person's sin over his head and force him to clean himself up to earn our love. Sure, the husband would be right to want his wife to demonstrate her commitment to the relationship again. But these actions must be a response to love and not a means of earning love.

God works this way. The psalmist asks, "If you, LORD, kept a record of sins, Lord, who could stand?" (Ps. 130:3 NIV). The obvious answer is "no one." We would not stand a chance if God made us earn our

> Forgiveness is the glue of relationships—without it they will never stick.

way into relationship each time we sinned. God doesn't keep a heavenly tally sheet to track whether our good deeds have been sufficient to merit His love. He simply loves and we respond to that love through our obedience.

The biblical word for this process is *reconciliation*. It's the idea that those who were once enemies become friends again. We might say that two boys who got in a fight on the playground were reconciled when they decided to forgive each other and team up in the two-on-two, after-school basketball game. Paul says that this is what God did for His children through Christ's work (see 2 Cor. 5:18). He took those who were estranged and enemies due to sin (God and man) and made them friends. Our human relationships are to demonstrate this heavenly reality.

Forgiveness is the glue of relationships—without it they will never stick. You may have heard the statement "Love means never having to say you're sorry." It may rival "Sticks and stones may break my bones but words can never hurt me" as the most foolish quip anyone has ever said. Love, in fact, means always having to say you're sorry. And love means having to extend forgiveness to those who say they're sorry.

Practicing forgiveness and forbearance is tough and will cost you a lot. But in Christ you not only have a model, you have a source for grace. He has forgiven you for more than you'll ever have to forgive anyone else, and you can pass that same grace to those who annoy and hurt you. Because of Jesus' sacrifice, we can bear with others and forgive them with no strings attached.

Unfortunately, many of us have been part of, or even helped build, communities where forgiveness was something to be earned in time through guilt, penance, and isolation. We must fight to resist this temptation. We must become groups where we don't retreat when our feelings are hurt, but where we consistently forgive and bear with one another.

Renie and I are working to establish these values in our children. When they sin against each other—which happens often—we have a three-fold way that we ask them to respond.

First, they go to the person they offended and tell what they did wrong. "I'm sorry" is not enough, but rather, "I'm sorry for stealing your toy and hiding it in the toilet." We want them to learn that confession means owning the wrongs that they have done. Second, they ask the person to forgive them: "Will you forgive me?" Third, give the offended kid a chance to answer "Yes, I will forgive you" and demonstrate this forgiveness with a hug. This process does not happen every time (some hugs turn into body slams), but we hope it instills in them a pattern that our kids will carry into adulthood.

A SINGLE TRAY

I met my wife in college. We got engaged six months after we started dating (I had to move quickly, otherwise she might have wised up). During our engagement, we were blessed to have numerous couples' showers/parties. I quickly learned that I was clueless about how to thank people for a gift when I had no idea what it actually was. I didn't know what a pot holder was, or why people gave us so many forks, spoons, and knives. I was naïve and would stupidly ask, "Why do we need all this silverware? Only two of us are getting married!"

It wasn't that I was ungrateful; I was just ignorant to the new life season that awaited me. There was one gift, however, that I will never forget opening. Leah, the lady who served as my administrative assistant and who'd been married for more than twenty-five years (almost forty years now), gave us a single food tray.

Wow, this is one of those luggage holders, I thought. *What's this tray doing with it? Shouldn't there be two? If we're both eating, who will get the tray?*

Leah explained that one tray serves as a reminder that we need to selflessly serve each other. Just as in life, often there are not two of every item that we need. Sometimes there is only one. I need to serve my wife by letting her have the tray even if that means I have to eat on my lap some nights. The reality is that marriage requires constant attention to the other person's needs.

Her point was well-taken. Through the years, Renie and I have learned that if we honor the other person in hopes of what we will get in return, we become more self-absorbed, but if we honor without any hope of receiving something in return, we will grow closer. To this day we keep that tray as a prominent piece in our bedroom, where it continues to remind us of what it means to honor each other.

That concept of honor translates well to how we should treat one another in community.

Honoring means that we willingly suffer for someone else's gain. Honoring causes us to value others more than our own comforts.

Though honor is not a word we often use when describing our everyday relationships, it should be something that permeates our communities, as the latter part of Romans 12:10 directs us: "Outdo one another in showing honor."

Paul's language here is startling. He doesn't want us simply to show honor, but to exceed how others show honor. The word *outdo* is a competitive word, something that requires hard work and struggle. The idea is that, rather than striving for the better yard, the better kid, the better marriage, or the better car, we should figure out how to make other people better. How can we love and serve them in such a way that makes them better, even if it makes us look worse?

TREAT LIKE THE GENERAL

The one place honor is modeled consistently is in the military. For instance, a private would do anything within his or her power to honorably serve the general.

Jesus was willing to suffer so that those who believed might gain life. In the same way, sacrificing for others is the heart of how a community operates. A military ranking mandate leads a private to honor the general, but within biblical community, the gospel compels us to honor, no matter the ranking. Our calling is to treat everyone as if he or she is a general.

When I was planting the church in Columbia, I would periodically take our leaders to conferences. I learned more during those trips by watching our people show honor to one another than I did from the world-renowned speakers on stage. We didn't have a lot of money so we would cram as many guys into a hotel room as we could. Each man would then argue his case for "getting" to sleep on the floor. It wasn't that the floor was a splendor of comfort, but these men wanted to show one another honor and were willing to *outdo* one another in this way. This virtue didn't merely show up during conferences. These men practiced it every day. They were the ones who laid the foundation for our church to build on.

We must build communities where we are willing to give up our preferences for someone else and to do whatever it takes to ensure that they have what they need. This is how a general would be treated.

But while a general has earned this right through hard work and years of military service, we treat people as though they have earned it all even if they haven't. You and I deserve nothing, yet in Jesus we have been given everything. When we practice the idea that *it's not about what I can get but what I can give*, we change people, both those who honor and those who are honored.

MISSION THREAD

Being part of a group who honors one another with no agenda is unlike anything the world has to offer. As outsiders get a taste of a community of sacrifice, they discover real security and hope. This directs people to the most amazing news the world needs: the gospel.

GETTING PRACTICAL

- **ARE** you willing to do the tough job of forgiving and reconciling?
- **DO** you always see "the tray" as something that is there for you?
- **ARE** you willing to drop everything for someone else?
- **DOES** even a slight inconvenience cause you to forfeit doing something for another?
- **IS** the front seat always necessary for you? Have you ever just thought about calling the backseat as you walk with a group toward the car?
- **ARE** dishes at the end of a good night with friends something you avoid or something you seek to handle?
- **WHO** can you honor this week? In what ways?
- **WHAT** are ways that you can consistently honor those in your gospel community?

"Rejoice in hope, be patient in tribulation, be constant in prayer."

—ROMANS 12:12

CHAPTER 9

PERSEVERING TOGETHER

I was sitting in a regular weekly meeting when my phone rang. The ID showed that Renie was calling. "It's my bride, guys. I'll be right back." I stepped from the room and answered the phone. On the other end came an eerie silence, and then sobs. My wife is not that emotional. I probably cry more than she does. So I knew something was seriously wrong.

"I'm here . . . in the parking lot," she finally choked out.

Immediately I ran outside, where I found Renie hunched over the steering wheel, weeping.

"There's no heartbeat!" she said as soon as she saw me. My wife was twelve weeks pregnant with our second child. And she had experienced a miscarriage.

We were heartbroken and confused. The air felt heavy with all our pain and unanswered questions. All we could do was embrace and cry together.

Then slowly we looked at each other and said three simple but powerful words: *God is good.* It didn't provide an insta-cure, but we both knew those words held the sustaining certainty we needed to hear and remember—and that we desperately needed our community to point us toward as the grief weighed us down.

While *God is good* is truth we live out as a community, we also need to be aware of three other undeniable words: *suffering is inescapable*.

SUFFERING IS INESCAPABLE

Misery comes in all shapes and sizes. It occurs at different times, places, and seasons. And we can be assured that we will not evade it. Tim Keller reminds us:

> Suffering is everywhere, unavoidable, and its scope often overwhelms. No matter what precautions we take, no matter how well we have worked to be healthy, wealthy, comfortable with friends and family, and successful with our career—something will inevitably ruin it. No amount of money, power, and planning can prevent bereavement, dire illness, relationship betrayal, financial disaster, or a host of other troubles from entering your life. Human life is fatally fragile and subject to forces beyond our power to manage. Life is tragic.[1]

Many believe that the gospel guarantees a life absent of affliction. If we follow the Bible, however, we know that this is simply not true. Pain is a regular part of a believer's life. As Bruce Milne writes: "Suffering is an essential ingredient of the Christian Life according to the unanimous testimony of the New Testament writings (1 Peter 4:13, Philippians 1:29, 3:10, 2 Corinthian 4:10f, 1:5, Romans 8:17, Colossians 1:24, Revelation 1:9)."[2] No matter how faithful we are, following Christ does not promise to be easy or pleasant. Frankly, it may be the opposite. Jesus assures His followers that "in the world you will have tribulation" (John 16:33).

Within our communities, people will lose jobs, succumb to diseases, end relationships, and suffer disappointments. We do not get a choice—trials *will* come. And in these moments we must remember the truth of the gospel, which testifies that God is always at work, even when we cannot see it and do not understand it.

GOD'S INVISIBLE HAND AT WORK

During seasons of suffering God's care works much like a sock puppet dancing before a captivated two-year-old. To the toddler, the dog, giraffe, or bear has come alive before his eyes. He doesn't grasp what any adult knows without a moment's thought: underneath that giraffe is an invisible hand orchestrating the rhythmic movements and silly motions. The child doesn't yet have the mental faculties to understand that there is more to reality than simply what he can see.

When we suffer—when all we see is the sock puppet—we need to remind one another of God's invisible hand at work behind the scenes, orchestrating all things for His good purposes.

The Old Testament book of Ruth is a good example. Ruth, a young Moabite woman, marries into an Israelite family. Over time, her husband, brother-in-law, and father-in-law die, and a terrible famine falls on the land. So she finds herself traveling with her mother-in-law, Naomi, back to Naomi's hometown, Bethlehem.

Naomi, bitter and broken, holds only one hope: that someone from her family will provide for her. She needs a kinsman-redeemer. But behind the scenes in the midst of this suffering we see God's sovereign hand at work. Ruth goes in search of food and "just so happens" to glean from Boaz's field—the very one who can redeem her and her mother-in-law. Then it "just so happens" that Boaz returns to his fields at the time Ruth is working. And it "just so happens" that he notices her. And it "just so happens" that he gives her an abundance of food to take home. And it "just so happens" that he is drawn to her, and ultimately redeems her through marriage.

You get the point: nothing "just so happens." Behind all that occurred in Ruth's life, God gave glimpses of His work in ways that she would have never understood at that time.

Perhaps you have had similar experiences with sorrow. Then years later you looked back on that situation and could note the multitude of ways God was faithful. You may even see how He deepened your love and trust for Him in ways that you would have never experienced had you not walked through that suffering.

The problem is that we forget. In our affliction, we are prone to lose focus on these brilliant truths. This is why community is vital. Others remind us of God's continued work in our lives and that we never suffer alone.

TOGETHER IN SUFFERING

When life brings trials that I cannot control, I quickly feel trapped. Instead of leaning in to my community, I tend to isolate myself.

Do you ever run from others when burdens weigh you down? This seclusion most often leads to frustration, which leads to anger, which eventually brings bitterness. Show me a bitter person and I will show you someone who does not truly allow others to walk with them in their pain.

But the truth that everyone suffers provides a unique point of contact (and common ground) for biblical community. The fact that everyone else also knows grief can allow me to be vulnerable with my pain and available to love others in the midst of theirs.

A few years ago I was part of a diverse community of guys. We had doctors, pastors, former homeless men, mechanics, and engineers. When one of the men shared about some deep-rooted childhood pain, he ended his story by saying, "But that's my own burden to bear." Not only was his story painful, but that he thought he had to carry it on his own was even more heartrending.

That night those men began to carry his burdens.

In Romans 12:12 Paul tells the community to "rejoice in hope, be patient in tribulation, be constant in prayer." We cannot do these things well apart from the church. This is particularly true in our suffering. It is disastrous to hurt alone; it is too great a burden. But in this passage Paul offers three ways that the church can best support those who suffer. Let's consider how each of these work within the context of our relationships.

1. Rejoice in Hope

The Christian community allows us to rejoice in hope. James says to "consider it pure joy, my brothers and sisters, whenever you face trials of many kinds" (1:2 NIV). These commands seem counterintuitive at best, and downright foolish at worst. There was zero that my wife or I wanted to *rejoice* in or *consider pure joy* when we learned that we were not going to have the baby we so desperately desired. So how could we rejoice in the face of such a broken, pain-filled world?

The answer lies in the object of Paul's rejoicing: hope. Hope is the basis on which Christians find joy in the midst of anguish. Writing to a church coming to grips with the death of believing saints, Paul wrote for them not to "grieve as others do who have no hope" (1 Thess. 4:13).

Christians have hope, while those apart from Christ do not. We know that this life is not all we see. We know that "the sufferings of this present time are not worth comparing with the glory that is to be revealed to us" (Rom. 8:18). This is our hope.

It is the Christian community's job to come alongside those languishing under the weight of trouble and remind them of this glorious hope. When we suffer alone, we become nearsighted.

Imagine driving down the interstate on a beautiful summer day. Ahead you see a line of clouds alerting you to a coming storm. As your car moves into the storm, you slow down, turn on your windshield wipers, turn off your radio, and focus on what's before you (or at least that's what you should do). At that moment, you are not focused on the destination but simply on surviving. Suffering can have this same effect. We fixate on our circumstances, so we need others to remind us of the hope that awaits us on the other side of the storm.

This is the church's voice to those struggling under a broken marriage, job loss, cancer, and the like. They need to know that God is still in charge, He is not shaken, and He is active.

A word of warning: you may have seen Christians offer this hope in the form of a platitude. In an attempt to provide hope without coming alongside, they are quick to say, "Brother, don't be sad. It's all going to work out." These trite statements do more harm than good.

First, we must understand that there is a time for listening and a time for speaking. We must know when to sit quietly and listen to those who are broken. In the moments following a tragedy, tears and silence may be better than words. In due time, God will give us opportunities to speak. And when He does, we must speak truth and not pop-Christian sentimentality, such as "God will work everything out." The idea behind the statement is that if the person simply holds on long enough, God will restore their health and their fortunes. But this is not always the case. Sometimes the hope we cling to is that God will work all things out "in the end."

Barry was part of our church when he was in high school. At an early age, he tragically lost his dad, and then through much of teenage years, he watched as his mom battled cancer. One night Barry invited a few of us from the church to pray with him and his mom. Earlier that day, the hospice staff had told Barry that his mother had only a few days to live.

That night about a dozen of us gathered in their home around her makeshift hospital bed. Jay, one of our staff who was a strong part of Barry's community, said, "Can I say something?"

The atmosphere was heavy, and Jay looked at Barry and his mom, and with tears welling in his eyes, he said, "God is going to heal."

Brother, I thought, *you don't throw something like that out there right now.*

Then Jay repeated it, this time more boldly and confidently: "God is going to heal." A smile formed as he continued, "God is going to heal you here and now, or when you see Him face-to-face. But either way, we can all rest in that truth as we pray. God will heal."

Jay spoke clear truth. And that truth carried great hope.

A couple days later, Barry's mother, who loved Jesus, was healed. No longer was cancer in her body, but she gained a new body as she passed into eternity.

During the visitation, Barry clung to that certainty as he told person after person, "God has healed my mom and she is with Jesus." God used community to speak a hope-drenched truth that Barry could anchor to.

2. Be Patient in Tribulation

Suffering is rarely a short-term phenomenon. When it is most salient, it feels as if it will go on forever. Paul tells us to "rejoice in our sufferings, knowing that suffering produces endurance, and endurance produces character, and character produces hope, and hope does not put us to shame, because God's love has been poured into our hearts through the Holy Spirit who has been given to us" (Rom. 5:3–5). The way we handle affliction as communities is fundamental in reflecting the gospel, but it is also vital to how we grow in the gospel. Trials bring the opportunity to grow as a community—in knowing, serving, sacrificing for, and ultimately loving one another well.

A young couple in a local church had a child born with severe disabilities. Multiple times during the child's first days, the parents weren't sure he would survive. While his birth had been difficult, the challenges compounded because the doctors didn't know what was wrong. They had no clear medical option to correct the problems. These parents were in for a long journey and they knew it. The next several years brought no easy answers, long nights with a sick child, emergency trips to the hospital, and unstoppable tears.

This couple, and scores of others, needed the church to come alongside them to help them persevere. Perseverance is that sense of long-suffering, staying the course, being faithful even when everything else is falling apart.

Clearly this is not something we can do alone. Our natural tendency is to get out of suffering as quickly as we can. But since not all trials are relieved that easily, we need the church to stick by us and exhort us to faithfulness so that we do not allow the pain to push us away from God.

We provide this support through our words and our actions. Our words remind others to stay connected to God in His Word and prayer, challenge others when we see areas of self-reliance, and encourage others to cling to God.

Our actions lighten the load to make it easier for our brothers and sisters to endure. Couples, like the one we mentioned, are more likely to persevere when their church family cooks them meals, cleans their home, sits at the hospital while one parent naps, and offers other tangible acts of service. As we do this, we send the message, *You are going to make it through this because we are walking with you.*

3. Be Constant in Prayer

The church also serves others by continuously praying. Too often we treat prayer as our last resort. Once we have exhausted all other means of providing tangible support, we might say, "Well, I guess all we can do now is pray." This statement reflects an impoverished view of prayer that dominates the church.

Prayer is not the last thing we do for others and that others do for us—it is, in fact, the most important thing. We have the amazing grace-gift of being able to intercede on someone's behalf.

Paul's command is not simply that people should pray. He tells us to be *constant* in prayer. This is one area where we could likely all use some prodding. I know that I am often prone to respond to someone who is hurting with a casual, "I'll pray for you." Sometimes I do. Often I don't. Rarely do I unceasingly pray for them.

Constant prayer provides a rich source of encouragement. We can do better than broad, sweeping social media appeals or the vagueness of unspoken prayer requests. Rather, we can let people know our specific needs and trust them to actively pray for God's grace and sustenance.

To pray like this, we must have a plan. I don't know about you but I'm not smart enough to remember everyone's needs. Even when I want to pray, I quickly forget. So I keep a prayer journal and a note system on my phone to remind me of what and how to pray. I can then serve my brothers and sisters in the most important way: through constant prayer.

SUFFERING AND OUR PRESENT GROWTH

These keys—rejoicing in hope, being patient in tribulation, and praying consistently—are the basis of grieving well in community. And they are the fires under which community is actually forged. In fact, the path of pain makes community with God possible. And not any pain, but the greatest act of anguish: the cross of Jesus Christ. Through His suffering, people can be united to God. In the same way, brothers and sisters can be united to one another in Christian love unlike what they could experience in any other way.

> Suffering is the God-appointed means of conforming us to the image of Jesus.

After reminding the church that they are to find joy in the midst of suffering, James states that this happens when a person knows that "the testing of your faith produces steadfastness. And let steadfastness have its full effect, that you may be perfect and complete, lacking in nothing" (James 1:3–4).

Sounds great, doesn't it? We all want to be complete and not lacking in anything. The seemingly bad news is that the path to completeness is pain. You and I simply will not mature if we do not suffer. Suffering is the God-appointed means of conforming us to the image of Jesus. Our trials are tools in the hands of a loving God who wants to make us and our churches look more like Christ. Thank God we do not have to suffer alone.

SUFFERING AND OUR FUTURE GLORY

Healthy communities understand that our table here is temporary and pales in comparison to the grand banquet table we will one day gather around.

My wife and I honeymooned in Hawaii. Friends gave us their timeshare to use in Oahu and SkyMiles to get there. We took a quick flight from South Carolina to Atlanta, and then an almost five-hour flight from Atlanta to Los Angeles. When we arrived at Los Angeles, we discovered that our five-and-a-half-hour flight to Hawaii had been delayed. Since we needed to eat dinner, we figured this would work out well.

But our terminal was under construction, so unfortunately, all the restaurants were closed. There we sat—for three hours—with a small bag of barbeque potato chips and a flat ginger ale.

My frustration level rose higher when they announced that the delay would be even longer. Finally Renie looked at me and said, "Please don't forget that this is only a layover. We are flying to paradise."

One of the best gifts our communities give us is the reminder that one day we will stand with God Himself. One day there will be no more suffering, no more disease, no more pain, no tears—none (Rev. 21:4). When heaven is our home, our communities can be ready for whatever life may give or take.

MISSION THREAD

Hope is a profound, though often neglected, tool in the church's missionary arsenal. The fact that all people suffer provides the church a unique point of contact with the nonbelieving world. They will suffer, lack hope, and fail to persevere. The Christian, in contrast, has hope, the means to persevere, and a constantly praying community of people. This allows us to present a compelling alternative to how the world deals with suffering.

When the world asks, we must speak of the good news that gives us hope: that God is at work in our pain. We can do better than simply saying, "I'm doing okay." We must speak of the final victory that is assured for those who are in Christ. We must speak of the reality that no pain can ever separate us from the love of God that is in Christ Jesus our Lord.

GETTING PRACTICAL

- **IN** what ways has your suffering uniquely prepared you to love and serve others?
- **HOW** can you boldly demonstrate the hope of the gospel to those outside the church?
- **WHAT** opportunities are you squandering to speak of the hope that is yours in Christ?

Life in Community

"Contribute to the needs of the saints . . ."

—ROMANS 12:13

CHAPTER 10

MEETING NEEDS

Recently I saw a social-media update from a well-known pastor of a growing church. This pastor shared about a homeless man who was living behind a gas station near the church building. A person from his congregation began picking the man up on Sundays for their service, and eventually the man got saved, was baptized, and became a member.

This is the wonderful part of social media. I loved reading this man's salvation story and the role the local church played in that. But then the unfortunate side of social media took hold. As everyone within the social-media thread was overjoyed for this man's salvation, their answer to his immediate physical needs were only wrapped around praying for his next steps—not theirs. *I hope he gets a home. . . . I pray for shelter. . . . Let's together pray he gets off the street. . . .*

As I thought of them hoping things would get better for this homeless man, my response worked its way into an outright rant:

You care for this man's salvation, but as soon as it costs you something, you turn to God and ask Him to fix it. This man is now part of your church and you are going to continue to bring him to your air-conditioned building, where his only "bath" in months was in your baptismal pool, and then you have the audacity to take him back to the alley behind a gas station. I bet you now call him "brother," and yet you will let him sleep in an alley as though he is a stranger. *Are you kidding me, church?*

First off, my comments to my four office walls were prideful, drenched in self-righteousness, and definitely not centered on a significant care for that local church—especially since I had been in a similar experience (which I'll get to later in the chapter).

I felt that they had missed, as I have often done, what God gave to us as responsibility. This man went from being a stranger to being a brother, and with that he brought a lot of needs to his new church family. This man's next steps should no longer be taken alone. He now walks a path that is biblically designed to be with his new family.

> If we believe the gospel, then we don't have to pray about helping those in our community with their needs.

I don't know the conclusion of the story (another unfortunate side of social media). For all I know the epilogue could be that this church has since helped this man into a house and is meeting every physical need while helping him pursue a sustainable lifestyle. My point is not to rant about a specific church, but to set the stage for understanding the idea of meeting the real needs of those we call family.

If we believe the gospel, then we don't have to pray about helping those in our community with their needs. Instead in Romans 12:13, Paul gives us clear instructions about how we should respond: "Contribute to the needs of the saints."

CORRECT PERSPECTIVE

When my team and I first moved to Columbia, South Carolina, to start a church, we did it intentionally to see a city changed. Our first season of ministry was filled with meeting city leaders and discovering the needs of our surrounding neighborhoods. We soon discovered that homelessness was a major issue that had never been proactively dealt with. The city's efforts had been reactionary at best. So to respond to that need, we began doing what we, as a bunch of twentysomethings, knew how to do: we threw parties.

Yes, you read that correctly.

We threw parties on street corners and in parks. We played games, ate together, talked about life, provided haircuts, listened, donated clothes, and did whatever we could to show the homeless that we wanted to be their friends.

During this season we experienced an amazing transformation. And it all came about through a meek and simple man named Luis.

Originally from Chihuahua, Mexico, Luis had been living as a nomad for eight years. He moved to this country with his family to discover a better life, but that life eventually became one of abandonment and addiction. Not long after being in the States, Luis's wife took their two daughters and left him. Luis was now alone—in a country where he barely knew the language. Luis was devastated and had nowhere to turn, so he tried to alleviate the pain with alcohol.

By the time we met Luis, he could no longer afford convenience-store alcohol and had turned to rubbing alcohol to get his "fix." He was homeless and slept in a dumpster.

A group of college students from our church discovered him and began to simply hang out with him. Not long after, they got him to attend church, and soon he became a Sunday-morning regular. These students lived out what the apostle Paul talked about in 1 Thessalonians 2:8: "We cared for you. Because we loved you so much, we were delighted to share with you not only the gospel of God but our lives as well" (NIV).

Soon Luis became a Christian. He was no longer a friend we hung out with every now and then; he was our family.

For several weeks I found myself in a similar situation to the church I mentioned earlier. I simply prayed that the Lord would help Luis get off the streets, but deep down I knew that his needs had become our community's needs. Neither the church nor I had a lot of money. Our offerings at that point were not much more than twelve dollars and a bag of Skittles. And worse, I really didn't want to be inconvenienced. While I was overjoyed for Luis's salvation and inclusion into our community, I wasn't ready for it to cost me anything.

Then one day my bold and soft-spoken friend Brandon came to me with tear-filled eyes. "Luis is not just my friend, he is my brother," he said. "And it is never okay for my brother to sleep in a dumpster. *This changes today.*"

God speaks boldly through His Word and often uses people like Brandon to direct us to what God Himself has made clear through the Scriptures. Brandon's words not only changed the story of homelessness in our city, but it impacted me personally as I began to see people through the eyes of Christ.

We made some calls, and that night one of our church families welcomed Luis into their home. Within weeks we found Luis his own place—completely furnished, including custom artwork in Spanish, and with stocked refrigerator. We helped him secure a job. And he was on his way to a sustainable lifestyle.

On moving day, Luis was so excited. He told us, "I have such a big family. Thank you! Now when can we do this for someone else?"

Not only did Luis progress from no home and no family to a self-sustaining lifestyle with a big family—he also began actively helping others who were in need. It was as though the Holy Spirit infused into his spirit what the theologian Dietrich Bonhoeffer wrote about: "God himself taught us to meet one another as God has met us in Christ."[1] And what Paul wrote in Romans 15:7: "Welcome one another as Christ has welcomed you, for the glory of God."

The gospel changed Luis's heart and God used his redemption story to remind us that the same gospel that frees us from our sin also makes us a family who meets one another's needs. When strangers move from being friends to becoming family, our perspective and then our efforts to meet these needs will radically change. I'm not suggesting, by the way, that we aren't called to meet the needs of those outside our family—that's part of the community's job on mission. But how can we hope to help strangers when we can't even help those who *are* family?

MAKE A PLAN

I didn't grow up in Tornado Alley, but the schools I attended in South Carolina regularly practiced tornado drills. We would line up along the infinitely long hallway and awkwardly sit with our backs against the lockers, holding our books against the top of our heads, and placing our chins all the way to our knees. This was about as comfortable as the position they would place you in for school photos. Nonetheless we were anticipating devastation to come our way, and so we practiced our plan of action.

Sure enough, when I was in seventh grade, the clouds turned an eerie grayish-green, the winds whipped the pine trees lining the back of our school, the rain flew sideways, and the alarm sounded—and this time it was not a drill. One thousand middle-school students entered the hallways in the center of the school, sat against the locker-lined walls, drew our knees to our chins, and held books over our heads. Everyone knew what to do and did it.

Let's be honest, middle school is somewhere between herding cats and organizing chaos, but in this moment it worked. Fortunately, the storm missed our school by a couple miles, and what could have been mass chaos was a calm and active group who knew exactly what to do.

At some point storms *will* hit the people within our community. The only question that remains: Is there a plan to meet those needs?

- When the people in your gospel community cannot pay their grocery bills, what do you do?
- If someone is struggling with a deep-rooted sin and doesn't need to be alone, where can they stay?
- When a single mom loses her real-estate job and has used up her savings, who steps up and helps her rebuild her resume?
- If cancer takes over a three-year-old girl's kidney and the family has no means to cover the never-ending medical costs, what do you do?

The above scenarios are real circumstances that I've seen in just the last couple years and our church has had to act quickly.

As I write this chapter I'm sitting in a loft that a family in my former church appropriately named The Retreat. I've recently felt as if I've hit a wall in a number of areas and have had the growing physical and spiritual need for some time away from the norm.

You may be thinking, *Wow, that's nice that a family has given up their loft for the weekend so you can have some rest.*

That *would* be gracious, but they planned their generosity long before my need arose.

When Mr. and Mrs. Smith became empty nesters, they decided to move from the suburbs into the city. They took the excess they could have used for their own spoils and strategically set that money aside to meet the needs of others within their gospel community. They bought two lofts: one to call their home and the other to call The Retreat—a place to provide people with rest and rejuvenation.

They gave me the door code, a card for the garage, and ultimately the weekend I needed. I had no idea what to expect at this loft, but I found a well-furnished escape with great food (three cartons of moose tracks ice cream were the highlight).

I tell this story not to point out the price tag of their investment but rather to show the heart that led the Smiths to strategically make provision to meet real needs. I am not naïve enough to believe that we can perfectly plan for every need that arises. But I do believe we can be strategically purposeful in how we make provision. Look at what this Scripture has to say about being intentional.

> When you reap the harvest of your land, you shall not reap your field right up to its edge, neither shall you gather the gleanings after your harvest. And you shall not strip your vineyard bare, neither shall you gather the fallen grapes of your vineyard. You shall leave them for the poor and for the sojourner. (Lev. 19:9–10)

The principle here is simple: everything we create and earn is not just for us. We are deliberately to share our blessings. This concept shows up again in the New Testament.

All who believed were together and had all things in common. And they were selling their possessions and belongings and distributing the proceeds to all, as any had need. And day by day, attending the temple together and breaking bread in their homes, they received their food with glad and generous hearts, praising God and having favor with all the people. (Acts 2:44–47)

The above passage beautifully shows the collective generosity of the church, which was a means by which everyone's needs were met. Note that everyone was involved. We are not on our own. We must work together to pull this off.

WHATEVER IT TAKES

A girl in our church consistently missed school and was late to work because the public transportation in the city did not run anywhere near her home. She needed reliable transportation. Some fellow college students with whom she walked in community decided to do something about it. At first the girls made legitimate excuses about how as college students they were limited in what they could do. But as they discussed it, one of the girls quoted Jesus and decided to be obedient to His calling: "Sell your possessions, and give to the needy" (Luke 12:33).

Over the next five months this group of six young women sold personal items on Craigslist and eBay and collectively threw the money in a jar. The jar became a large bowl and the bowl became a bucket, and the money in that bucket eventually bought a $6,000 car for a girl in need. Not only did they help one of their family members, but the act itself cemented their bond and encouraged them to look for other opportunities to help. Very simply, their obedience to God's call changed them.

These young women did not sit passively and watch this girl lose her job or have to quit college. They made a *whatever it takes* plan and went to work. Their actions not only changed them, but within months our entire church's culture undertook a massive shift. Our other communities began to purchase vehicles. A struggling family whose car blew up received a minivan within a few days. A single mom whose transmission fell apart had a new car within a week, along with a check to cover the insurance and a gift card to purchase gas for an entire year. We did not form a committee or set up a fund. The point was not cars; it was a no-excuses posture for meeting needs.

As gospel communities we must do whatever it takes to intentionally meet the needs out of an overflow of God's grace. And a lost and hurting world will take note.

MISSION THREAD

People who will actually sell their possessions to give to those in need, who live as the church we see modeled in the Bible, mesmerize a cutthroat, dog-eat-dog society. This is the sort of community that shines bright in a dark world. It is God's design and it's time that we "contribute to the needs of the saints."

GETTING PRACTICAL

- **WITHIN** your church, who have needs that you could help meet?
- **WHAT** holds you back from meeting those needs?
- **IT** will probably cost you something. What are you willing to give up? Is there any inconvenience you are not willing to face?
- **WHO** can partner with you?
- **STORMS** will come, and when they do, is there a plan?
- **HAVE** you cut back or set aside so others may reap the benefit of your mindful planning?

Life in Community

". . . Seek to show hospitality."

—ROMANS 12:13

CHAPTER 11

PURSUING HOSPITALITY

Early in our marriage, Renie and I had dinner with an older couple who were building a house. They explained that their key objective was to design something comfortable for guests, because they wanted to serve others not just "in the world," but inside their home.

I was blown away. I'd always wanted to build a nice house that suited my needs, where I could escape from the world. But what if our homes were meant to be places of retreat and comfort for others as well?

Throughout this book we've discussed the value of authentic, Christian community. What better place to pursue loving other people than in our homes?

THE MISSION OF HOSPITALITY

The notion of hospitality was far more common to the people in Jesus' day than it is to us. At that time people who traveled were at the mercy of others to provide them lodging and meals. For example, when Jesus sent His disciples out to proclaim the gospel and heal diseases, He told them to look for hospitality. If the disciples were welcomed and given care, they were to stay and serve. If they were not, then they were to move on and shake the dust off their feet as a sign of God's judgment on that town (Matt. 10:14; Luke 9:5).

To early Christians, the home was a place to extend grace to others. This should be true of our homes as well. What better way to demonstrate the hope of the gospel than to invite others into our homes where they can hear it proclaimed and see evidence of a transformed life.

Too often we view our homes as places of refuge rather than tools to advance the gospel. My friend Michael Rhodes stated, "Christians can be generous with their time and money but stingy with their homes. We must repent from worshiping the comfort of our homes. . . . Life will change for you when your home becomes a hub of hospitality rather than a hotel for the healed."[1]

Hospitality gives us the opportunity to display the gospel to those we welcome into our homes, whether it's those who are a part of our community (see 1 Pet. 4:9) or those we want to see experience true community (see Heb. 13:2). Let's say after a rough day of work, you get home to discover that your spouse invited the new socially awkward neighbors for dinner. Your home provides a wonderful way to build a relationship that might otherwise be impossible. This couple may not know God, so they can observe you love each other and love them while you talk about God's grace. Or they may have a relationship with God but have never experienced biblical community. A friendly conversation, a nice meal, and the warmth of a home make relationships far easier to form.

> Hospitality is the practical outworking of the gospel into the rhythm of our everyday lives.

Hospitality welcomes people into community—which is what Jesus modeled in His kindness toward us, as Paul points out in Ephesians 2:12–13: "Remember that you were at that time separated from Christ, alienated from the commonwealth of Israel and strangers to the covenants of promise, having no hope and without God in the world. But now in Christ Jesus you who once were far off have been brought near by the blood of Christ." Jesus gave Himself for us even when we were outsiders with no interest in being a part of His family. He moved on mission into our world and made us community by inviting us inward to His table.

Your home can either feed seclusion or counteract it. The goal here is not to build a big house in the name of hospitality. The aim is to use whatever home God has given you. If you are in a dorm room or a two-hundred-square-foot city loft or a five-thousand-square-foot home in the 'burbs, you can still pursue hospitality.

I've seen college students, living in a room the size of most pantries, excel at hospitality. Their rooms were places of warmth, joy, and welcome for all who lived on the hall. People knew that if they stepped into those rooms, they would be loved. As a result, these rooms were where everyone wanted to be.

In Romans 12:13, Paul simply and clearly tells us: "Seek to show hospitality." The phrase *seek to show* or the word *pursue* (in the HCSB translation) is the idea of a continuous action. Life is rhythmic and Paul argues that hospitality is the practical outworking of the gospel into the rhythm of our everyday lives. We practice hospitality when we consistently receive others into our lives and homes in the same fashion as Christ received us.

A SIMPLE INVITATION

When our family moved to Atlanta, our daughter was eight weeks old, our son was two, and in the metro area bursting with six million people, my wife and I had exactly zero friends. We were dying for even a hint of biblical community. A guy at work invited me to play golf (which I never turn down), but really I accepted because I was desperate to meet anyone.

He invited two others who worked in our organization, but I had not met either one. I ended up in a cart with Micah. He was extremely competitive and took the game a little too seriously, so I knew I was going to get along with this guy. Micah talked about his family and how they had only been in the area for a year. At the end of the round Micah asked me, "Do you guys have a lot of friends here?"

"Nope, not at all," I told him.

Two hours later I was putting his address into my phone. Micah and his wife, Laurie, invited our family to his home that night for dinner. Unbeknownst to us, their home was one street over in the same neighborhood as our house. It took us approximately thirty-nine seconds to make the long drive.

When we arrived that night we immediately felt at home. They loved us, cared for us, had mature conversation with us, and invited us into their lives. It was an answer to prayer.

To this day Micah and Laurie are the people we walk most deeply with in community. Our kids play together, break things together, and fight together. We have spent the last two years confronting one another, confessing to one another, and seeking to join together to display the gospel in our neighborhood. A simple invitation into their home has grown our love for Jesus and our involvement in everyday mission.

For Renie and me, it was the move to Atlanta that prompted us to use our home to do a better job of making friends and forming biblical community. I realize you may be hardwired to do this more naturally than others. If you're an extrovert, you thrive on having people around. The thought of hosting a houseful of guests to entertain makes you come alive. But you may be an introvert and this whole idea makes you want to hide in your room under your pillow.

> The home is the greatest environment that exists to create and cultivate community.

Hospitality is not only for certain personality traits, however. If you're an introvert, you must not use your personality as an excuse to ignore God's call. If you're an extrovert, you must make sure that your goal is pure. I know some extroverts who invite people over to make themselves feel loved and affirmed rather than to serve others. Though our personalities will shape how we apply hospitality, all people can pursue it by recognizing these six key truths.

SIX PRACTICAL TRUTHS

The home is the greatest environment that exists to create and cultivate community. But how do we "do it right"? The first thing is to understand what hospitality is and is not.

1. Hospitality Is Not about Entertaining

What have you historically thought about when you hear the word *hospitality*? Rachel Ray, Martha Stewart, *Southern Living*, cleaning, cooking, setting the table, coordinating colors, Pinterest, plate arrangements, table decorations?

This perception of hospitality means providing a flawless menu, an unsurpassed environment, and the perfect conversation. It's like trying to provide the magical experience of Disney within the confines of your home. This ideal carries with it a load of pressure, and when you feel that crushing weight, you are not practicing biblical hospitality—you are entertaining.

Entertaining isn't about loving people. It's about impressing people. And trying to impress people isn't loving them. It's loving yourself. There is distinct difference in entertaining and hospitality. One falsely builds up self, while the other is drenched in the sincere love of Romans 12:10 (which we discussed in chapter 8).

Author Jen Wilkin offers clarity between the eerily similar but vastly different practices:

Entertaining vs. Practicing Hospitality

- Entertaining is always thinking about the next course. Hospitality burns the rolls because it was listening to a story.
- Entertaining obsesses over what went wrong. Hospitality savors what was shared.
- Entertaining, exhausted, says, "It was nothing, really!" Hospitality thinks it was nothing. Really.
- Entertaining seeks to impress. Hospitality seeks to bless.[2]

The gospel says the pressure is off. You're freed to love people because there's no need to impress them. You don't have to give folks Disney World every time you open the doors of your home. Give them you.

This doesn't mean you can't attempt to make good food. That's a great way to serve people. If you can't cook well, order takeout. Don't poison anyone with your lack of culinary skills—that's not entertainment or hospitality, that's just wrong. It also doesn't mean you shouldn't wipe down the table so it's clean enough to eat on. That's something you should do regardless of whether or not you understand Jesus-centered hospitality.

But—and this is an important *but*—the excuse, "We can't have people over, the house is a mess!" is no longer valid. Can I let you in on a secret? Most people have been in a house before. Many people even live in them, and they know houses get messy. It's okay for them to see evidence of everyday life. We're inviting folks into real life in a way that they get to know the real us, and feel comfortable enough to be their real selves, which leads to real community. Relax and let people see you and how God's grace meets you in your messy life.

2. Hospitality Is about an Open Life

Hospitality is about relational posture and attitude far more than any amount of skill, action, or practice. It's a heart that says, *Yes, there is room in my life for you.* This requires that you work to embody the values we have discussed in this book: you are open and honest, you bring your best to the table, you encourage one another with the goodness of God. These practices will allow others to feel welcomed through your efforts.

You could have an open house and not have an open life, but it is near impossible to have an open life and not have an open home. This is one area where you may be at an advantage if you are more introverted. Sure, you may not desire to have thirty people in your home every night, but what about building a relationship with one person? You can talk in greater depth rather than attempt the vast array of relationships that extroverts may desire. You, as an introvert, can go deeper while others, who are extroverts, can go wider.

3. Hospitality Is a Community Project

Share the load. It is much better when everyone pitches in, so no one individual or family has to foot the whole bill. Everyone can do the dishes so the host isn't left with them at the end of the night. We get to use what we've been given (see chapter 4) to team up. Does your house or apartment not have enough space? No problem, work with someone in your community who does. Do you lack organizational skills or time to call and invite people? Great, partner with someone who has what you lack.

Hospitality is a community endeavor. God has sovereignly placed you with the people you are around so you can team up in your efforts. Every shortcoming you have is an opportunity for God to provide through someone else.

God's call for us to be in community isn't separate from His call for us to live together on mission. As we mentioned before, it's two sides of the same coin. Community and mission intersect perfectly in the value of hospitality. Throw a cookout together and invite neighbors or coworkers and watch God work. Make this a regular practice.

4. Hospitality Can Be Planned or Spontaneous

Whether you are a type-A planner or a fly-by-the-seat-of-your-pants personality, you can make hospitality a regular part of your life. Renie and I practice both planned and spontaneous get-togethers. Every week we try to have people into our home. We strategically budget our time, energy, and money to do this. But we will also spontaneously call people at 5 p.m. and ask them to join us for dinner.

Renie and I make sure to check with each other first to ensure that we don't miscommunicate, but if we're sure the night is free, why not? A quick phone call and we can obey Paul's challenge to show hospitality. Our kids often play in the front yard, and through that we tend to strike up a lot of conversations with neighbors that may end in a meal together. Both Plan A and Plan B work great, and Hebrews 13 tells us not to neglect showing hospitality, because it's not going to happen on accident. So pick your path and do it.

5. Hospitality Is Powerful

In chapter 8 we discussed loving one another, based on Romans 12:10. Just three verses later we arrive at the command to pursue hospitality. Both Hebrews 13 and 1 Peter 4 carry a similar literary pattern, which states to love one another and then moves toward practicing hospitality:

> Let brotherly love continue. Do not neglect to show hospitality to strangers, for thereby some have entertained angels unawares. (Heb. 13:1–2)

> Above all, keep loving one another earnestly, since love covers a multitude of sins. Show hospitality to one another without grumbling. (1 Pet. 4:8–9)

The pattern is that showing genuine love leads to offering hospitality—both for those in our community and for strangers outside our community. It even says in Hebrews 13:2 that "some have entertained angels unawares." The writer of Hebrews is referencing two Old Testament events where Abraham and Lot practiced everyday hospitality (see Gen. 18 and 19). They met strangers and offered them food, protection, and relationship. In both cases they subsequently dined with angels, and in the occasion of Abraham (Gen. 18), numerous scholars contend that this is one of the rare instances in the Old Testament when Jesus appeared in the flesh.

In the midst of everyday hospitality you have no idea what God might seek to do.

You may think, *So the Bible says angels—and maybe even Jesus—are going come to my house? This sounds awesome! I'm in.* No, that's not what the Bible says. The writer of Hebrews is saying that in the midst of everyday hospitality you have no idea what God might seek to do. In one sense, hospitality is the easiest biblical command to obey. Just open your home, right? But it is also the easiest to overlook because of its seeming simplicity and lack of value.

You may wonder, *I share good food, have some laughs, and then I have to clean way more dishes than the norm. So what significance and power does hospitality really carry?*

Can you think of a time when you were somewhere new and somebody made you feel truly welcome? It's incredible, right?

When I entered my freshman year of college, I was extremely insecure (I covered it with pride) and lonely (I covered it with an obnoxious arrogance), and I really just wanted to belong.

Matt, a sophomore I met the first week at a campus event, invited me to his apartment to hang out with other college students, eat pancakes, and watch a movie. Matt wasn't trying to do anything grand, he simply loved Jesus and wanted to put the gospel on display through the simple act of inviting others into his home. I just happened to be one of those "others."

What Matt did was more powerful than he knew. He didn't entertain angels that night (quite the opposite), but he altered the trajectory of eight college guys' lives. From that point forward, that group, with Matt as our leader, lived in intentional community—and it all started with pancakes, an open life, and an open home.

Sixteen years later I still share deep community with many of these brothers, even though we are scattered all over the world. When I face a big decision, these men are some of the first people I call. When I need prayer, I lean on them and know they actually and consistently pray. When I hurt, I call them to grieve. When I have something to celebrate, they are the first guys I call. Community is not based on proximity, but intentionality—and that intentionality often begins through hospitality. Hospitality is more powerful than we can imagine.

6. Hospitality Is Worth the Sacrifice

Peter tells us to "show hospitality to one another without grumbling" (1 Pet. 4:9). Hospitality will always cost us something, whether it's money, time, energy, peace, or quiet. It's easy to grumble because it can be a sacrifice.

But it's also worth it.

A young couple decided to walk their neighborhood every night to meet their neighbors. Over time, they got to know Ted and Barb, who were first-time parents. Ted and Barb tried everything to get their baby to sleep—from incessant walks in the stroller to driving around the block over and over, hoping the car engine's rhythmic hum would help.

The young Christian couple noticed Ted and Barb's efforts, and having four kids of their own, remembered what it was like with that first baby. They also knew that young parents are always tired and the last thing most of them want to do is cook.

So they offered hospitality. "Hey guys, we know you have a little one and cooking is probably a real challenge. We'd love to have you over for dinner one night," they said. This simple act was the key to unlock a relationship, as that meal allowed the couples to commiserate about parenthood and even talk about some best practices for getting a baby to sleep. Before long, Ted and Barb asked why this couple had cars in their driveway every Thursday night.

"Oh, that's when we do small group," they answered. "We'd love to have you join us."

Ted and Barb did join them. They heard the gospel and ultimately placed their faith in Jesus. All of this happened because of intentional hospitality.

As gospel communities we are called to give up the isolated view of our homes. By pursuing hospitality, we grow from a self-focused, self-centered way of life and use our homes as a tool for displaying the gospel.

MISSION THREAD

People drive alone to work, sit alone in an office, eat alone, drive home alone, and watch TV alone, all while our neighbors do the same things. Hospitality is a God-given means of addressing the loneliness that plagues our culture.

GETTING PRACTICAL

- **WHAT** night of the week could you commit to invite someone into your home for a meal?
- **DO** you know your neighbors' names? What would it take for you to learn their names and something simple about them?
- **WHAT** would it take for you then to offer them hospitality?
- **WHO'S** the new family on the block? Is there a new coworker? Could you invite them to dinner?
- **HOSPITALITY** is a great way to provide a tangible blessing (a warm meal) and a source of encouragement (a warm conversation) to those who are broken. Who around you is hurting?

SECTION 3

NEXT STEPS FOR STRONG COMMUNITY

"Do not be slothful in zeal, be fervent in spirit, serve the Lord."

—ROMANS 12:11

CHAPTER 12

DO SOMETHING AND START NOW

S teve felt alone. Once happily married, he was now thirty-one, divorced after learning of his wife's ongoing adultery, and a single dad. He felt crushed.

Sadly Steve's involvement with the family of God consisted of casual, Sunday-morning attendance and superficial ministry involvement. He went to church but never truly experienced biblical community. Now when he needed it most, he was isolated from the very people who could serve as God-given gifts to bolster his faith, meet his needs, and bear his burdens.

How could the principles in this book help someone like Steve? What would change if he saw the church as a family rather than as an institution?

In a word: *everything*.

If you remember, this book started out with a weighty word: *loneliness*.

Now I'd like to introduce another powerful but more profound word: *belong*.

Belonging stands in opposition to loneliness. It shows us that we have a place at God's table.

GRACE CAPTURES OUR HEARTS

Our God is good. As we have seen, He is not idle; He lovingly enters our story of brokenness, makes us whole and new, and invites us to dine with Him. This is not simply the story of a father who invites His child to leave the kids' table and join the big-people's table. Although endearing, and I have heard—and even given—that illustration many times, nonetheless it is about as accurate as the answers my three-year-old would give on a trigonometry exam.

Without Christ we are not sitting at *any* table. We are outside the house as an enemy, lying lifeless on the street. Jesus leaves what is comfortable to seek His enemies—not to kill them but to breathe life into them. How many stories do you know where the hero seeks out his enemy, grants him life, and then shares a meal with him? This is our story. This is the story of the gospel. We miss the truth of grace if we believe we have earned or deserve to be at His table.

Jesus meets our desperate need for salvation and then gives us a place within gospel community, where our loneliness is gone and our desire to belong is fulfilled. Grace is a tantalizing story of scandal, where seemingly impossible needs are met and the greatest invitation ever is given.

GRACE MOTIVATES OUR ACTIONS

Imagine people who love one another enough that they will not allow any need to go unmet, that they will be truthful enough to confront and encourage each other no matter the cost. Picture a community that collectively finds joy even in the midst of tragedy. This is what happens at a table marked by love: cities transformed by the simple obedience of a small group of Christ-followers who put others' needs above their own.

Can you see it?

A table where people bring their wins, their losses, their burdens, their tears, their gifts, their questions, and their pains while serving others who bring their wins, their losses, their burdens, their tears, their gifts, their questions, and their pains. It's a beautiful table to belong to and to give to.

Visualize the opportunities of what could be and should be: uncountable gospel communities spread across Seattle, Toronto, Belo Horizonte, Sydney, the suburbs of Dallas, Dubai, countrysides, and your own town—loving one another and serving the neighbors that God has placed them around. The loneliness that runs rampant in the lives of millions can change—all because a grace-filled community lives beyond itself and points to the One who is greater. This is what God has called us to.

> This is what happens at a table marked by love: cities transformed by the simple obedience of a small group of Christ-followers who put others' needs above their own.

This type of community is possible, but we must zealously pursue it. Unfortunately, I believe too many Christians are bored. One of our greatest plagues is apathy. The monotony of the church is not for a lack of modern flashy lights, swoopy-haired worship leaders, or entertaining, jeans-wearing preachers, but rather an absence of people aggressively seeking the community and mission of God together. We are not called to sit still; we are called to eagerly join God in what He is doing and wants to do in and through our communities. The day of boredom should be over and the inactivity of our churches must end.

In Romans 12:11, Paul exhorts us: "Do not be slothful in zeal, be fervent in spirit, serve the Lord." We will not accomplish this challenge in a church building for one hour on a Sunday morning. It requires far more than that. Biblical community happens "out there"—in the places where you and I do life every day. Movement is vital. "Never be lacking in zeal" means not to be stagnant.

My dad has had back pain for as long as I can remember and was forced to retire on disability when he was in his early fifties. This was tough for my father to deal with because he had been in carpentry work since he was ten years old. He'd had multiple surgeries with no success, and a couple years ago he had an extremely dangerous and invasive surgery that seemed more experimental than anything.

After five grueling days in the hospital, he was released to go home. The physical therapist gave him specific activities to do if he ever wanted to become active again. But instead he remained in bed day after day.

I'd phone my mom for a progress report, and each day she'd say, "He didn't move again today." He was growing weaker and becoming more frustrated. The surgery he had hoped would give him a better life was sending him into a downward spiral.

During one visit he asked the doctor if something else could help him—a new brace or a special medication?

Finally, his doctor told him, "You are never going to progress until you get over yourself, get up, and decide to do something about it."

I'm not sure Dad was the happiest camper after those remarks. But after a few days, he got up and tried to move.

That day I called my mom and asked to speak with him.

"He's gone on a walk," she informed me.

When I let out a sarcastic laugh, she insisted, "Really, he took a few steps this morning that turned into a walk down the stairs, out the back door, across the yard, and to the barn."

Dad had not just taken two or three steps; he had taken more than six hundred! His muscles woke up—not because of some miraculous drug, but simply because he moved. No longer was he sluggish, but rejuvenated. If my dad had remained inactive, his body would have continued the landslide, as his muscles would have slowly died. Muscles are designed to be in motion.

What does this have to do with biblical community? Simply put, it's time for us, as the doctor prescribed, to get over ourselves, get up, and decide to do something about it.

SLOTHFUL AND STAGNANT

When I was in high school I drove a 1987 Chevrolet Blazer with a 2.5-liter engine. Not long after I got the car, I discovered this stench that occurred every time I turned on the air. As much as I tried, I couldn't figure out where it was coming from or why.

Apparently water runs through the cooling system, which must eventually move its way out. Have you ever noticed the small pool that forms under a car on a hot summer day? That is merely the water flowing through the system, as it should.

I finally discovered the source of the car's smell: the pan was clogged and the water never moved as it was designed. It sat stagnant.

If we just show up and do nothing, we will kill our mission.

In a moment of true Southern ingenuity, I used a good old fashioned power drill and formed new holes in the pan. Immediately, the water drained and within days my car no longer smelled.

It's the same with the church. If we just show up and do nothing, we will kill our mission. Rather than filling the world with the aroma of Christ, we will give off the stench of death. As A. W. Tozer states:

> One year sitting around sulking will do more to rust your soul than 100 years of hard work, if God granted you that many years. . . . The devil always finds something for idle men and women to do. There is danger in idleness. So let us walk circumspectly and not be idle. . . . Woe to the idle Christian. He will not grow in grace.[1]

Has your apathy led to spiritual atrophy? The cure can be as simple as taking a step. Whether it is a step of confession, encouraging another, meeting a real need, or anything else God may motivate you to do, put your foot on the floor, join with your community, and take it.

GRACE-DRIVEN EFFORT

We do not live morally or serve passionately as a means of earning anything, but rather we bless as an overflow for what God has so graciously given to us. We err gravely when we believe that morality is Christianity. Our motivation is not the by-product of just feeling good internally, it comes from the actual inward transformation (see Rom. 12:2).

God's grace moves into our soul through the power of the cross and the Holy Spirit's conviction. That grace then motivates us to build community and live on mission. Theologian D. A. Carson calls this "grace-driven effort."[2] This type of effort is part of Paul's challenge to us in the last part of Romans 12:11: "Be fervent in spirit, serve the Lord." Grace-driven effort, coupled with an accurate perspective on what gospel community is about, changes everything.

PLAN OF ACTION

Our communities must be intentional, which means we must pro-actively work to bring and welcome people to the table. Answer the following questions and see where God may be working to transform you and your community.

1. What is God telling you about your role in community?
2. What are you going to do about it?
3. What community value is most challenging for you to apply? Why?
   - Embracing and using gifts
   - Sincerely loving
   - Confronting
   - Confessing
   - Biblically encouraging
   - Honoring
   - Practicing joy, patience, and prayer during painful times
   - Meeting real needs
   - Pursuing hospitality
4. With whom can you discuss the above questions?

5. What marks of community do you long to experience?

6. What barriers are between you and your desired state?

7. What must you do to knock down the barriers and take steps now?

GRACE TO YOU

Remember Steve from the beginning of this chapter? This recently divorced man raising a one-year-old son, crippled by loneliness that he did not choose, decided to pull up a chair to the table. Rather than sitting passively in a church building each week, he did the hard work of moving out of anonymity and into relationships. One night he took a risk and showed up at a small group meeting. He took the first step and community did the rest.

He entered a home filled with laughter, joy, and food! Rather than condemnation, he received love. Rather than cowering in shame, he discovered open fellowship. Rather than living in isolation, he found community at the table. That night, Steve shared the story of his broken marriage and his wounded heart. He wept tears of regret. He lamented the journey that he feared awaited his son. He agonized over his constant loneliness.

And that night Steve found that he was not alone. People prayed over him. They begged God to change his wife's heart and bring her back. They reminded Steve of the hope of the gospel: that while he felt alone, God had not abandoned him.

But it did not stop that night. Over the next weeks, months, and years, the church came alongside Steve and found meaningful ways to bear his burdens. They cooked meals, painted his home, and kept his son so he could have a break. In some ways, Steve gained a far bigger family than he ever lost.

This is what God's table offers each of us. God bids us to do everything we can *as a community* to see to it that as many people as possible have the opportunity to experience a place at His table. God pursued us—and for most believers, His pursuit came through another person who already had a seat at the table.

The time is now. You and I may never meet in this lifetime, but I look forward to sitting at the table with you on the other side of eternity. Until then, let's do something and start now.

Life in Community

LEADER'S GUIDE: SIX-WEEK STUDY

HOW TO USE THIS GUIDE

Life in Community seeks to display how community is formed, what it practically looks like to apply the biblical values (Rom. 12:1–13) of community to everyday life, and in what ways community puts the gospel on display.

The goal of this book is not to get you into a group but to help you build true community. However, groups do tend to be a great framework for community to take place. It only makes sense to discuss and process the idea with other people with whom you are doing life. The hope is for missional communities, small groups, Sunday school classes, church-plant core teams, entire churches, and church staffs to work through the book together and allow it to shape the way they build community.

This study guide is intended to be a supportive resource for any leader or group facilitator. I have provided a "Tips to Leading" resource and then a simple, straightforward guide for the six-week study.

TIPS TO LEADING A
LIFE IN COMMUNITY
SMALL GROUP

1. Journal through the assigned Bible chapter for the week.
Study the assigned chapters intently. Consult simple commentaries like the *Bible in Easy English* (www.easyenglish.info) to add insight to the original meaning and context of the passages.

2. Pray. Answer all nine questions as part of your prep. Then pray that God will go deeper in others who are in community with you.

3. Leave room for other voices. The first level of group conversation is you talking to the group. The next level is that the group talks back to you. The third level is the group talks to each other. When God talks to people, the group is functioning on the highest and healthiest level.

You talk > We talk back > We talk to each other > God talks to us

4. Start your formal group time by connecting. Be creative and have fun. Give the group something easy to talk about before moving into "Heart Matters."

5. Watch the clock. Because of the open-ended approach to these questions, the deeper the conversations the greater the time challenge.

- Clearly identify your end time at the beginning of the formal meeting.
- Let people answer questions one-on-one and in triads.
- Decide in advance how much time you will spend on each section.
- Designate a group timekeeper.
- Keep moving. Conclude the meeting before they become aware of the clock.

6. Review the past week's debrief. Coach your group toward action. Reviewing next steps from the last gathering raises accountability for hearing God and following through. Have participants pray for each other concerning their next steps.

7. Become a great listener. Listen to what God says to you about others. Listen beyond what is normal and comfortable for you.

8. Be creative. Anything can get boring, even highly engaging approaches to group learning. If you are not creative, find someone in your group who is and let them help you.

SMALL GROUP STUDY
WEEK 1

BEFORE THE GROUP GATHERS, HAVE EVERYONE READ:
- *Life in Community*, chapters 1 and 2
- Ephesians 2

HEART MATTERS
- What do you normally substitute for community?
- What personal barriers have you created to community?
- What unhealthy ways have you processed loneliness in your past?

SOUND BITES
"Communities centered on the gospel fly in the face of isolation and yet convey the grace-filled inclusion that we so desperately desire. These communities bring with them the answer the world is hungry for. It is a community that invites others to feast at the Lord's table." (*Community*, p. 29)

"The universal need for a Savior, a true source of living water, gives us the correct awareness to find common ground and is foundational to forming a healthy community." (*Community*, p. 40)

ZOOM IN
Ephesians 2
- What key verses or phrases from this passage speak to living in community?
- What verse did God want you to see/hear/apply?
- What verse would be a great gift for someone close to you?

DEBRIEF

- What benefits of community would help you most now?
- What adjustments would you need to make to give space for community?
- What steps will you take in the next thirty days to make those adjustments?

SMALL GROUP STUDY
WEEK 2

BEFORE THE GROUP GATHERS, HAVE EVERYONE READ:
- *Life in Community*, chapters 3 and 4
- Philippians 2

HEART MATTERS
- What scares you most about living in community?
- What are some advantages to not living in community?
- What attracts you most to living in community?

SOUND BITES
"The table is not a table for one. It's an enormous banquet table where God Himself invites all to come and dine." (*Community*, p. 69)

"Going at it alone is not the path for a disciple of Jesus. Through grace we don't just belong to Christ—we also belong to one another." (*Community*, p. 52)

ZOOM IN
Philippians 2
- How does this chapter reinforce the value of community?
- What verse did you need most?
- How could you shape that verse into a prayer?

DEBRIEF
- In what area do you need the greatest transformation?
- How can living in community help you in that area?
- What steps will you take in the next thirty days to let others support you?

SMALL GROUP STUDY
WEEK 3

BEFORE THE GROUP GATHERS, HAVE EVERYONE READ:
- *Life in Community*, chapters 5 and 6
- 1 John 4

HEART MATTERS
- Where are you the most tempted to put on a mask?
- What part of your heart does God need to change to help you become more honest?
- What are the pros of being completely honest in community? the cons?

SOUND BITES
"The depth believers experience with one another is linked directly to their level of honesty. Any relationship built on the façade of lies will surely crumble over time." (*Community*, p. 81)

"I'm not suggesting we create sin police who constantly bust people in their depravity. I am, however, encouraging us to become a people who love one another enough to hate the things that hurt us." (*Community*, p. 90)

ZOOM IN
1 John 4
- What key verses or phrases from this passage speak to loving in community?
- What verse did God want you to see/hear/apply?
- How can you make the verse a part of your week?

DEBRIEF

- How can you help create a culture of honesty in your community?
- How can you become a safe person to whom people make risky confessions?
- Who is the safest person to whom you can make a risky confession in the next thirty days?

SMALL GROUP STUDY
WEEK 4

BEFORE THE GROUP GATHERS, HAVE EVERYONE READ:
- *Life in Community,* chapters 7 and 8
- Romans 12

HEART MATTERS
- What person do you struggle being positive about?
- Who do you need to speak more directly to?
- What is the biggest change God has made in you over the past year?

SOUND BITES
"Biblical encouragement uses your words to point out examples of God's goodness in another person's life." (*Community,* p. 107)

"As we become people who see life as a gift and not something we are entitled to, we will view people through a completely different lens. And as we grow deeper into the depths of God's mercies, we will discover that our life is also given to us to be given away to others." (*Community,* p. 118)

ZOOM IN
Romans 12
- What is your most pressing question about this passage?
- What verse did God want you to see/hear/apply?
- What verse could you give as an encouragement to someone else?

DEBRIEF

- Who do you need to affirm this week?
- How will you affirm them?
- What steps will you take in the next thirty days to be more encouraging?

SMALL GROUP STUDY
WEEK 5

BEFORE THE GROUP GATHERS, HAVE EVERYONE READ:
- *Life in Community,* chapters 9 and 10
- James 1

HEART MATTERS
- What trial are you currently experiencing?
- How can your group help?
- What is God changing in you through this challenge?

SOUND BITES
"Suffering is the God-appointed means of conforming us to the image of Jesus. Our trials are tools in the hands of a loving God who wants to make us and our churches look more like Christ. Thank God we do not have to suffer alone." (*Community*, p. 135)

"If we believe the gospel, then we don't have to pray about helping those in our community with their needs." (*Community*, p. 140)

ZOOM IN
James 1
- What part of the passage was the hardest for you to accept or understand?
- What verse did God want you to see/hear/apply?
- What part of this passage gives you courage in spite of personal challenges?

DEBRIEF
- Who in your world is going through a trial?

- What can you do this week to make a meaningful connection with them?
- How can you more fully engage a need in your city over the next thirty days?

SMALL GROUP STUDY
WEEK 6

BEFORE THE GROUP GATHERS, HAVE EVERYONE READ:
- *Life in Community*, chapters 11 and 12
- 1 Peter 4

HEART MATTERS
- Who models hospitality well?
- What do they do that you admire most?
- What resources do you have that you struggle the most to share?

SOUND BITES
"The aim is to use whatever home God has given you. If you are in a dorm room or a two-hundred-square-foot city loft or a five-thousand-square-foot home in the 'burbs, you can still pursue hospitality." (*Community*, p. 151)

"Grace-driven effort, coupled with an accurate perspective of what gospel community is about, changes everything." (*Community*, p. 168)

ZOOM IN
1 Peter 4
- What is your most pressing question about this passage?
- What verse did God want you to see/hear/apply?
- How does this chapter apply to sharing your life with others?

DEBRIEF
- Which of your neighbors needs hospitality from you this month?

- What are your next steps to make this goal a reality?
- What is one thing God has convinced you to do as a result of your *Life in Community* study?

NOTES

Chapter 1: The Need for Community

1. http://www.newsweek.com/lonely-planet-isolation-increases-us-78647.

2. Ibid.

3. Taken from his personal Twitter account (@rickwarren) on October 31, 2014.

4. Tim Chester and Steve Timmis, *Total Church* (Wheaton, IL: Crossway, 2008), 74, 56, 65.

5. http://toddengstrom.com/2013/04/15/stages-of-missional-community-development-team-of-missionaries/.

Chapter 2: Common Ground

1. D. A. Carson, *Love in Hard Places* (Wheaton, IL: Crossway, 2002), 61.

2. http://www.pewforum.org/2011/12/19/global-christianity-exec/.

3. Edward T. Welch, *When People Are Big and God Is Small* (Glenside, PA: P & R, 1997), 45.

4. Harris III, *The Illusion of More* (Shippensburg, PA: Destiny Image, 2014), 30.

5. Danny Akin, in a message delivered at Send North America Conference, July 30, 2013.

6. Timothy Keller, *Gospel in Life Study Guide* (Grand Rapids, MI: Zondervan, 2010), 192.

7. Dietrich Bonhoeffer, *Life Together and Prayerbook of the Bible* (Minneapolis: Augsburg Fortress, 2004), 34.

Chapter 3: Continuously Transformed

1. Neil Postman, *How to Watch the TV News* (London: Penguin, 1992), 1.

2. David Platt, in a message delivered at Send North America Experience Tour, September 8, 2014.

Chapter 4: Your Best at the Table

1. C. S. Lewis, *Mere Christianity* (New York: HarperCollins, 2009), 185.

2. You can access a free and simple survey through www.lifeincommunity.com/assessment. Or check out some tests through http://www.lifeway.com/lwc/files/lwcF_MYCS_030526_Spiritual_Gifts_Survey.pdf.

Chapter 5: No Masks Allowed

1. Original source unknown.

2. Donald Miller, *Scary Close* (Nashville: Nelson, 2014), xv.

3. http://www.desiringgod.org/sermons/let-love-be-genuine.

4. Joseph H. Hellerman, *When the Church Was a Family* (Nashville: B & H, 2009), 1.

Chapter 6: Hate Can Be a Good Thing

1. http://www.desiringgod.org/sermons/abhor-what-is-evil-hold-fast-to-what-is-good.

Chapter 7: Glue to the Good

1. Sam Crabtree, *Practicing Affirmation* (Wheaton, IL: Crossway, 2011), 17.

2. Ibid., 12.

3. Mike Robbins, *Nothing Changes Until You Do* (Carlsbad, CA: Hay House, 2014), Chapter 7.

Chapter 8: Love, Like, and Honor

1. Illustration inspired by John Piper. http://www.desiringgod.org/sermons/love-one-another-with-brotherly-affection.

2. C. S. Lewis, *Mere Christianity* (New York: Macmillan Publishing/Touchstone Edition, 1996), 116–117.

Chapter 9: Persevering Together

1. Timothy Keller, *Walking with God through Pain and Suffering* (New York: Penguin, 2013), 1, 3.

2. Bruce Milne, *We Belong Together* (Downers Grove, IL: InterVarsity, 1978), 34–35.

Chapter 10: Meeting Needs

1. *Life Together and Prayerbook of the Bible*, 25.

Chapter 11: Pursuing Hospitality

1. http://sendnetwork.com/2014/10/28/everyday-neighborhood-missionary/.

2. http://jenwilkin.blogspot.com/2013/11/choose-hospitality.html.

Chapter 12: Do Something and Start Now

1. A. W. Tozer, *The Dangers of a Shallow Faith* (Minneapolis: Bethany House, 2012), 118, 120, 124.

2. http://www.thegospelcoalition.org/blogs/gospeldrivenchurch/2010/05/28/grace-driven-effort/.

ACKNOWLEDGMENTS

This book has been in the works for many years. The content first started to take shape when I was a freshman at Clemson University, where I first experienced true community. It has grown during my years as a church planter with the crew at Midtown in Columbia, South Carolina, and has matured with the people with whom I now live on mission in the Atlanta area.

The process of getting all these thoughts and experiences inked has been a community effort, and I am grateful to the people who have given so much to *Life In Community*.

Renie: You have sacrificed so much in our twelve years to spread the gospel, build community, and advance God's mission. I am constantly encouraged by the grace you give to me, to our kids, and to others who gather at our table. You lead the way in hospitality and continually show me what walking in humility should look like. I love you, and I am grateful for the gift you are and the support you have been to this work.

Jack and Piper: There is no better sound than walking in the door and hearing both of you yell "Daddy" as you run as fast as you can to tackle me. I want Jesus for both of you more than anything in this world. Thank you for caring about this book—your simple words of *You can do it, Daddy* have kept me going. I love you, and pray I get to watch you lead the next generation in advancing God's church in the world.

My Family: Pa, Ma, Mandy, Wendy, Joey, Michael. Thank you for the way you display the gospel through your love for other people and your consistent sacrifice to love one another. The example you have set for me is foundational to the message in this book. Maddie, Will, Ben, Gracie, and Janie. It is my constant prayer that you will experience the joy of following Jesus and joining His mission. Frank, Cindy, Merritt, Jeff, and Kate. Thank you for welcoming me to your table and giving me the privilege of calling you family.

Clemson Family: Matt New, Allen Tipping, Dave Thomas, Brad Jones, Nathan Tidd, Paul Coleman, Chris McGowan, Dustin Hughes, and the rest of the Clemson group. Thank you for introducing me to what community could and should be.

Midtown Family: Jay Hendricks, Lee Cunningham, Brandon Clements, Michael Bailey, Kent Bateman, Michael McFadden, Ryan Rike, Chris Kakaras, Jon Ludovina, Adam Gibson, Allen Tipping, and the rest of the Midtown group. Thank you for creating a culture centered on Jesus, His family, and His mission. The content of this book was gleaned from your teaching and friendship.

Atlanta Family: Andrew Kistler, the Beegees (Vince and Darlene), the Millicans, the Critsers, and the Bucks. Thank you for allowing us to build community with you and the support you have given during this writing process.

NAMB Family: Kevin Ezell, Carlos Ferrer, Joe Outlaw, Aaron Coe, Matt Martin, and the Board of Trustees. Thank you for your guidance and support in allowing me to pursue this project and the freedom you have given me to follow my passion to write. I am extremely grateful. The rest of the NAMB Crew—I could not work with better people. You're the best.

David Platt: Thank you for the humility in which you lead and your belief in the message of this book. I am grateful for your friendship and appreciate the inspiring words you added to this work.

Ginger Kolbaba: Your ability to pull out the message I am trying to say is uncanny. Thank you for your constant encouraging words and your ability to cut ten thousand words in the ninth hour.

Matt Rogers: Thank you for your friendship and partnership in ministry and the countless hours you helped me think through this work. You are a wordsmith who makes me so much better at this craft.

Brandon Clements: I am grateful to have you as a brother. Your thoughtful critiques and additions to this book have made it much better. Thank you.

Dino Senesi: You are the ultimate coach who has always been loyal to me. Thank you for helping me shape powerful questions that will help lead communities toward transformation.

Landon and Jordan Thompson: Not only did you guys capture the amazing photo on the front of this book but you also continue to display what mission looks like in your city. Thank you for being missionaries who often pose as artists and photographers. The church in North America needs more people like you.

Kent Bateman: Your creativity and willingness to always bring things to life through graphics are a gift. I'm grateful for your friendship.

Joshua Rainwater: Your willingness to step in and capture part of the story of this book was a major help toward the vision of this project coming to completion.

The Von Fanges: Your generosity in giving me the time and space to complete this book was priceless. Thank you.

The Team at Moody: Thank you for taking a chance on me and believing in the message of this book. Duane Sherman and Parker Hathaway—It is an honor to call you friends.